Webster's

First

Picture

Dictionary

Compiled by Blaine Howard

Edited by Susan Kantor

BCL Press • New York

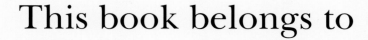

This book belongs to

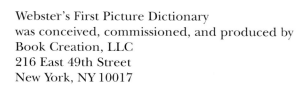

Webster's First Picture Dictionary
was conceived, commissioned, and produced by
Book Creation, LLC
216 East 49th Street
New York, NY 10017

Compiler: Blaine Howard
Editor: Susan Kantor
Picture Researcher,
Editorial Associate: Megan Schade
Book Designer: Kevin McGuinness

Photography: Anatographica, LLC; Belden Hill Picture Library; Church Street Photo Archives; Corbis®; CPG Picture Library; Photodisc®.

Cover and interior illustrations © 2001 Kevin McGuinness

ISBN: 0681-92009-2

Printed and bound in China

01 02 03 04 LFA 9 8 7 6 5 4 3 2 1

Aa

able *adj.* If you are **able**, it means that you can do something.

*I am **able** to pour my own cereal and milk for my breakfast.*

about *prep.* **About** is having to do with something.

above *prep.* **Above** means to be on top of or over something.

*The balloon floated up **above** my head.*

accident *n.* An **accident** is something, usually bad, that happens by surprise.

across *prep.* **Across** means from one side to the other.

*I walked **across** the field.*

act *v.* How you **act** means how you behave.

add *v.* **Add** means to find the total of two or more numbers.

*The teacher said, "When you **add** two plus two, the answer is four."*

address *n.* (addresses) An **address** tells you exactly where a place is.

*The **address** of my grandma's house is 221 Stone Street.*

adult *n.* An **adult** is a grown-up person or animal.

*Cindy's father is an **adult**.*

adventure *n.*
An **adventure** is an exciting trip.

*Visiting the jungle is an **adventure**.*

afraid *adj.* **Afraid** is being frightened or scared.

*I used to be **afraid** of dogs.*

after *adv.* **After** means following someone or something.

*"C" comes **after** "B" in the alphabet.*

afternoon *n.* **Afternoon** is the time between lunch and dinner.

*The baseball game is at three o'clock on Sunday **afternoon**.*

again *adv.* **Again** means to repeat something.

*Please say your name **again**.*

against¹ *prep.* **Against** means next to, leaning on, or touching something.

*Ben is leaning **against** the lawnmower.*

against² *prep.* **Against** also means to be on the other side in a contest or sport.

*On Saturday, the New York Yankees are playing **against** the Boston Red Sox.*

age *n.* **Age** is how old someone or something is.

*On my next birthday I'll be seven, the same **age** as my cousin Tom.*

agree *v.* When you **agree** with someone, you think the same way about something.

*We **agree** that the party is fun.*

air¹ *n.* **Air** is what we breathe.

air² *n.* **Air** also means sky.

*Fran's kite is flying way up in the **air**.*

airplane *n.* An **airplane** is a machine with wings that flies quickly through the sky.

alive *adj.* **Alive** means living.

all *adj.* **All** means every person or thing.

*I put away **all** of my toys.*

almost *adj.* **Almost** means close to.

*We are **almost** home now.*

alone *adj.* **Alone** means with no one else, by yourself.

*Ben was **alone** in the house when the doorbell rang.*

along *prep.* **Along** means next to, or with something.

*We walked all **along** the river until it ended at the lake.*

alphabet *n.* An **alphabet** contains all the letters a language uses to make words.

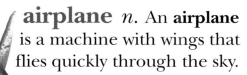

*The English **alphabet** has 26 letters.*

always *adv.* **Always** means every time.

*School **always** starts at 7:45 A.M.*

amount *n.* An **amount** is how much of something there is.

*The **amount** it cost was $2.50.*

angry *adj.* **Angry** is being mad about something.

*Andy was **angry** at Kate for going to the show without him.*

animal *n.* An **animal** is any living thing that is not a plant.

*The blue whale is the biggest **animal** in the world.*

another *adj.* **Another** means one more.

*May I have **another** cookie?*

answer *n.* An **answer** is a reply to a question.

*The **answer** to your question is yes.*

apart *adj.* When people or things are **apart**, they are away from each other.

*I stretched my arms far **apart**.*

appear *v.* To **appear** means to suddenly come into sight.

*The moon will **appear** at seven o'clock tonight.*

argue *v.* To **argue** is when two people think differently about something, and each one tries to make the other think they are right.

*Sometimes I **argue** with my friends about which TV show is best.*

armor *n.* **Armor** is a suit of metal worn for protection.

*King Arthur wore **armor** when he fought in battles.*

army *n. (armies)* An **army** is made up of soldiers trained to protect their country.

around *prep.* **Around** means on all sides.

*There were trees all **around** the lake.*

arrive *v.* **Arrive** is when you get to the place you are going to.

A B C D E F G H I J K L M

arrow *n.* An **arrow** is a straight stick with a sharp stone or metal point at one end.

Arrows are shot from a bow.

art *n.* **Art** is something made by people to be beautiful and interesting.

*Museums are made to hold **art**.*

ask *v.* To **ask** is to put a question to someone.

*Jason will **ask** his Dad if he can sleep over at Brad's house.*

asleep *adj.* **Asleep** means sleeping.

*Arthur fell **asleep** on his desk.*

attention *n.* **Attention** means watching or listening carefully.

*Pay **attention** to what the teacher is saying.*

audience *n.* An **audience** is a group of people who watch or listen to a performance.

*The **audience** clapped at the end of the show.*

aunt *n.* Your **aunt** is a sister of one of your parents, or your uncle's wife.

author *n.* An **author** is someone who writes books, plays, or poems.

*Dr. Seuss is the **author** of* The Cat in the Hat *and many other books.*

awake *adj.* **Awake** means not to be sleeping.

*Mom said I could watch the late movie if I could stay **awake**.*

away *adj.* **Away** means gone from a place.

*My cat went **away** one day and didn't come back for a week.*

Bb

baby *n. (babies)* A **baby** is a newborn or a very young person or animal.

*My aunt's **baby** was born two weeks ago.*

baby animals

chick

duckling

fawn

kittens

lamb

piglet

puppies

lion cub

N O P Q R S T U V W X Y Z

back *n.*
Back is the opposite of front.

bad *adj.* **Bad** means not good.
*The weather was so **bad** we had to play inside all day.*

bag *n.* A **bag** is a container for carrying things.

bake *v. (bakes, baking, baked)* **Bake** means to cook something in an oven.
*Mom will **bake** cookies for the party.*

baker *n.* A **baker** is someone who makes bread, cakes, pies, and cookies.

ball *n.* A **ball** is a round object that is used to play a sport or a game.
*Pete threw the **ball** into the basket.*

ballet *n.* **Ballet** is a kind of dance that tells a story.

balloon *n.* A **balloon** is a thin rubber bag. When it is filled with air and tied shut at one end, it gets bigger.

band *n.* A **band** is a group of people who play music together.

bandage *n.* A **bandage** is a clean covering used to protect a cut.

bank *n.* A **bank** is a place where people keep their money.

bark¹ *n.* The sound a dog makes is called its **bark**.

bark² *n.* **Bark** is also the covering on the outside of a tree trunk.

barn *n.* A **barn** is a large building on a farm where farmers keep their tools and animals.
*Josh went to the **barn** to milk the cows.*

baseball *n.* **Baseball** is a game that is played with a bat and a ball by two teams of nine players.

basket *n.* A **basket** is a container for holding, storing, or carrying things. Baskets are often made of woven wood, straw, or plastic.

bat¹ *n.*
A **bat** is a wooden or metal stick used to hit a ball.

bat² *n.* A **bat** is also a small mammal with wings.

bath *n.* When you take a **bath**, you wash yourself while sitting in a tub of soapy water.

beach *n. (beaches)* A **beach** is the sandy or pebbly land next to an ocean or lake.
*We build sand castles at the **beach**.*

beak *n.*
A **beak** is the hard part of a bird's mouth.
*The robin held a worm in its **beak**.*

bean *n.* A **bean** is an edible seed of a plant.
*I like chili with a lot of **beans**.*

beautiful *adj.* Something lovely to see, hear, or smell is often called **beautiful**.
*She played a **beautiful** melody on the piano.*

bed *n.* A **bed** is a piece of furniture to sleep on.

before *prep.*
Before means in front of or happening earlier than something else.
*Tina brushes her teeth **before** she goes to bed.*

begin *v. (beginning, began, begun)* **Begin** means to start.

*The play will **begin** when the audience is quiet and in their seats.*

behind *prep.* **Behind** means in back of something.

*Paul hid **behind** a tree.*

believe *v. (believes, believing, believed)* **To believe** is to feel certain that something is true.

*I **believe** he is telling the truth.*

bell *n.* A **bell** is made of metal and makes a ringing sound when it is hit.

belong[1] *v.* When something **belongs** to you, it is yours.

*Does that book **belong** to you?*

belong[2] *v.* To **belong** means to be in the right place or part of a group.

*The book **belongs** on the shelf.*

below *prep.* **Below** means under.

*Plants start to grow **below** the ground.*

bend *v. (bends, bending, bent)* If you **bend** something, it is no longer straight.

*The doctor has to **bend** down to check Tommy.*

beside *prep.* **Beside** means next to.

*I sit **beside** Ruth in school.*

best *adj.* **Best** means better than all of the rest.

between *prep.* **Between** means in the middle.

*The pink sponge is **between** the blue and green sponge.*

bicycle *n.*
A **bicycle** is a machine for riding. It has two wheels, handlebars, a seat, and two pedals.

big *adj.* **Big** means large.

*The mother horse is **big** compared to her baby.*

bird *n.* A **bird** is an animal with feathers and wings. Most birds can fly.

birthday *n.*
A **birthday** is the day of the year on which a person was born.

bite *v. (biting, bit, bitten)* To **bite** into something is to cut it with your teeth.

blanket *n.*
A **blanket** is a cloth cover used for keeping warm.

*In the winter, I sleep under more than one **blanket**.*

blind *adj.*
Blind means not able to see.

block[1] *n.* A **block** is usually a solid piece of wood or plastic with six flat sides.

*My brother built a castle with **blocks**.*

block[2] *v.* To **block** means to stand in the way.

*If you **block** the door, people can't get in or out.*

blow *v. (blowing, blew, blown)* **Blow** means to push air out of the mouth.

*Rob will **blow** up the balloons.*

boat *n.* A **boat** is a vehicle that travels across water.

*Some **boats** have engines and some have sails.*

N O P Q R S T U V W X Y Z

body *n.* *(bodies)* Your **body** is all of you—inside and outside.

*My **body** starts at the top of my head and ends at my toes.*

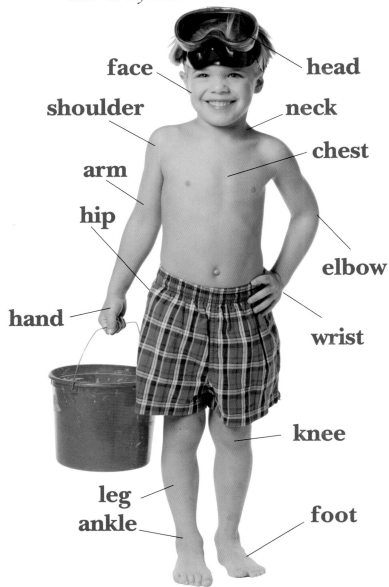

face
head
shoulder
neck
chest
arm
hip
elbow
hand
wrist
knee
leg
ankle
foot

bone *n.* **Bones** are the hard parts inside a body that make up the skeleton.

book *n.* A **book** is something to read. It has pages on the inside and a hard or soft cover on the outside. The pages are filled with words or pictures.

*Use these **books** for school.*

bored *adj.* **Bored** means not interested in doing anything.

*Tony is **bored** even though he has lots of toys, books, and games.*

born *v.* When a baby is **born**, it comes out of its mother's body.

*My baby brother was **born** last week.*

borrow *v.* **Borrow** means to use something that belongs to someone else for a while.

*I asked Will if I could **borrow** his bicycle since mine has a flat tire.*

bottle *n.* A **bottle** is a container that holds liquids.

bottom *n.* The **bottom** is the lowest part.

bow¹ *n.*
A **bow** is a kind of knot, with a loop on each side of it.

*Jill tied a big **bow** on the present.*

bow² *v.* **Bow** means to bend the top half of the body down.

*The actors **bowed** at the end of the play.*

bowl *n.* A **bowl** is a round, deep dish.

box *n.* *(boxes)* A **box** is a container used for holding or storing things.

__Boxes__ often are made of cardboard, wood or plastic.

boy *n.*
A **boy** is a young male. When a boy grows up, he will be a man.

brain *n.* The **brain** is inside the head. It is what lets us think, remember, move, and feel.

brave *adj.*
To be **brave** is to act unafraid.

*Josh was **brave** to defend his friend against the bully.*

bread *n.* **Bread** is a food made of flour and baked in an oven.

A B C D E F G H I J K L M

break *v. (breaking, broke, broken)* If something **breaks**, it doesn't work or can't be used.

*If you drop that glass, it will **break**.*

breakfast *n.* **Breakfast** is the first meal of the day.

breathe *v.* **Breathe** means to take air into the body through the nose or mouth and blow it back out.

*The air we **breathe** in the country is cleaner than the air in the city.*

brick *n.* A **brick** is a block of baked clay.

*The post office is built of **bricks**.*

bridge *n.* A **bridge** is a path built over water so people can cross from one side to another.

bright *adj.* **Bright** means shining and filled with light.

*Joe wears sunglasses when the sun is **bright**.*

bring *v. (brings, bringing, brought)* **Bring** means to carry.

*Please **bring** me the book from the table.*

broom *n.* A **broom** is a tool for sweeping. It has a long handle and a brush at the bottom.

brother *n.* A **brother** is a man or boy who has the same parents as you.

brown *adj.* **Brown** is the color of wood or chocolate.

*The chicken has **brown** feathers.*

brush *n. (brushes)* **Brushes** are tools made with bristles that are attached to a handle.

*I have a tooth**brush**, a hair**brush,** and a paint**brush**.*

bubble *n.* A **bubble** is a delicate ball of soap or water with a pocket of air inside.

bucket *n.* A **bucket** is a round container with an open top used for holding things.

*Tony's shovel is next to his **bucket**.*

build *v. (builds, building, built)* To **build** something is to put all the pieces of it together in the right order.

*My uncle knows how to **build** a house.*

building *n.* A **building** is a place with walls and a roof.

bulb *n.* **Bulbs** are big and round at one end, and thinner and straighter on the other.

*David put a new **bulb** in the lamp.*

burn *v.* If something **burns**, it is on fire.

*I like to watch the logs **burn** in the fireplace.*

bus *n. (buses)* A **bus** is a vehicle with lots of windows and rows of seats.

*We ride the **bus** to school every morning.*

bush *n. (bushes)* A **bush** is a plant with many branches that grows close to the ground.

busy *adj. (busier, busiest)* **Busy** means having a lot of things to do.

*Joel can't play because he is too **busy** with his chores.*

butter *n.* **Butter** is a food made from milk or cream.
*Jim likes **butter** on his bread.*

button *n.*
A **button** is a small round knob or disk on our clothes to keep them closed.
*My sweater has five **buttons**.*

buy *v. (buys, buying, bought)*
Buy means to pay money for something.
*We will **buy** a birthday present at the store.*

Cc

cage *n.*
A **cage** is a box with bars and a lock. Many animals are kept in cages.
*My aunt keeps her bird in a **cage**.*

cake *n.* A **cake** is a sweet food usually baked in an oven and served as dessert.

calendar *n.* A **calendar** shows the days, weeks, and months of a year.
*I circled everyone's birthday on the **calendar**.*

call[1] *v.* To **call** is to speak in a loud voice.
*The train conductor **called** "all aboard!"*

call[2] *v.* **Call** also means to talk to someone using the telephone.

camera *n.*
A **camera** is a machine for taking pictures.

camp *n.* A **camp** is a place where people can sleep outdoors or in tents.

can *v.*
Can means able to do something.
*Susan **can** ride a two-wheel bike.*

candle *n.* A **candle** is made of wax and string and burns to make light.

capital[1] *n.* A **capital** is the city in a state or country where its laws are made.
*Washington D.C. is the **capital** of the United States.*

capital[2] *n.* **Capital** also means the large letters of the alphabet.
*Sentences start with a **capital** letter.*

captain *n.* The leader of a team is often called a **captain**.

car *n.* A **car** is a machine with four wheels and an engine to make it go.

card *n.*
A **card** is a piece of stiff paper. Cards can be used for sending notes or for playing games.
*I got my report **card** in the mail.*

A B C D E F G H I J K L M

care *v.* To **care** about someone or something means you feel they are important to you.

*Aunt Jessie always sends me a birthday card because she **cares** about me.*

careful *adj.* If you are **careful**, it means you pay attention to what you are doing.

*Rita is **careful** when she crosses the street.*

carry *v. (carries, carrying, carried)* **Carry** means to pick something up and move it from one place to another.

*Karen **carries** a basket from the garden.*

cartoon *n.* A **cartoon** is a funny drawing.

castle *n.* A **castle** is a large building with stone walls and high towers.

catch *v. (catches, catching, caught)* **Catch** means to take hold of something while it is still moving through the air.

*Daphne can **catch** a ball in her glove.*

cave *n.* A **cave** is an opening in the side of a mountain or under the ground.

*Thousands of years ago, people lived in **caves**.*

cereal *n.* **Cereal** is a food made from grains like oats, wheat, and corn.

chair *n.* A **chair** is a piece of furniture you sit on.

chalk *n.* **Chalk** is a soft powdery stone made into sticks and used for writing and drawing.

chalkboard *n.* A **chalkboard** is a flat, smooth surface used for writing with chalk.

*Most **chalkboards** are dark green or black.*

change *v.* **Change** means to become different in some way.

*If you take ice out of the freezer, it will **change** to water.*

chase *v.* **Chase** means to run after.

*My dog likes to **chase** squirrels.*

cheap *adj.* Something **cheap** costs very little.

*I bought two pretzels because they were so **cheap**.*

cheerful *adj.* **Cheerful** means feeling happy.

*I felt **cheerful** after reading your card.*

cheese *n.* **Cheese** is a food made from milk.

***Cheeses** can be soft or hard.*

chest *n.* A **chest** is a large, strong box with a lid.

chew *v.* We **chew** food with our teeth to make it soft and small enough to swallow easily.

child *n. (children)* A **child** is a young boy or girl.

chocolate *n.* **Chocolate** is a food made from cacao seeds. It is usually sweetened with sugar and used to make candy and other sweet cookies.

choose *v. (chooses, chose, chosen)* To **choose** means to decide which one you want.

*Did you **choose** chocolate or vanilla ice cream?*

circus *n. (circuses)* A **circus** is a traveling show with clowns, acrobats, and trained animals.

city *n. (cities)* A **city** is a large town where people live and work.

clap *v. (claps, clapping, clapped)* **Clap** means to hit your hands together to show that you are pleased.

*I hope the audience **claps** at the end of our play.*

class *n. (classes)* A **class** is a group of students.

claw *n.* A **claw** is a very sharp, curved nail on the foot or paw of an animal.

The beaver has sharp claws.

clean¹ *v.* To **clean** means to remove the dirt from something.

*I use soap and water to **clean** the windows.*

clean² *adj.* **Clean** also means not dirty.

*I put on a **clean** shirt this morning.*

clear *adj.* **Clear** means easy to understand.

*It's important to have **clear** directions.*

climb *v.* **Climb** means to move up or down.

*The painter has to **climb** up and down the ladder.*

clock *n.* A **clock** is a machine that shows the time.

close¹ *v.* **Close** means to shut something or turn something off.

close² *adj.* **Close** means near to.

*We live so **close** to my school that I can walk there in two minutes.*

clothes *n.* **Clothes** are things people wear to cover their bodies.

t-shirt

shirt

belt

skirt

pants

socks

shoes

sneakers

cloud *n.* A **cloud** is a shape in the sky made up of millions of tiny drops of water.

coffee *n.* **Coffee** is a drink made from the roasted and crushed seeds of coffee plants.

coin *n.* A **coin** is a round piece of money made of metal.

cold *adj.* **Cold** means not hot.

color *n.* Red, yellow, and blue are the primary **colors**. You can mix them together to get all other colors.

*To get the **color** orange, mix red and yellow paint together.*

comb *n.* A **comb** is a tool for making hair neat.

I use a comb to get the knots out of my hair.

complete¹ *adj.* **Complete** means having all its parts.

The complete game is supposed to have dice, a board, and six play pieces.

complete² *v.* *(completed, completing)* **Complete** also means to finish.

You have five more minutes to complete the test.

computer *n.*
A **computer** is a machine that stores information and uses it in many ways to solve problems.

comfortable *adj.*
Something that is nice to be in or wear is **comfortable**.

Dad's big chair is really comfortable to sit on.

confused *adj.*
Confused means not sure.

Salma was confused by the directions.

container *n.* A **container** is something used for holding things.

continent *n.* A **continent** is one of the seven main bodies of land that make up the Earth. The continents are North America, South America, Europe, Africa, Asia, Australia, and Antarctica.

People in the United States live on the continent of North America.

continue *v.* **Continue** means to keep doing something.

Please continue reading until you finish the paragraph.

control *v.* *(controls, controlling, controlled)* **Control** means to be in charge.

The captain is in control of the ship.

cook *v.* To **cook** means getting food ready to eat.

When you cook carrots, they get soft.

cookie *n.*
A **cookie** is a small cake made from sweet dough.

cool *adj.*
Cool means almost cold.

Although it isn't winter yet, the air is getting cool.

copy *n.* *(copies)* A **copy** looks just like something else.

corner *n.* A **corner** is the place where two sides, lines, or roads meet.

correct *v.* To **correct** something means to get rid of any mistakes.

Diane needs to correct many answers on her test.

cost *n.*
Cost means how much you pay for something.

How much did your camera cost?

costume *n.*
A **costume** is a special outfit you wear so that you look like someone else.

Who is that dressed up in the clown costume?

cotton *n.* **Cotton** is the soft, white fiber from a **cotton** plant.

Cotton is used to make clothes, towels, and other things.

cough *n.* A **cough** is a sudden loud noise from the throat.

count *v.* To **count** means to figure out how many of something there is.
*Can you **count** all the people in the room?*

country *n. (countries)* A **country** is a land with its own laws, customs, and language.

couple *n.* A **couple** means two of something.

cousin *n.* A **cousin** is the child of a brother or sister of your parents.
*Aunt Marilyn's children, Kevin and Lucille, are my **cousins**.*

cover[1] *n.*
A **cover** is a top or a lid.
*Put the **cover** back on the soup pot.*

cover[2] *v.* To **cover** means to put something over another thing.
***Cover** her with this blanket.*

crab *n.* A **crab** is a sea animal that has a hard shell and eight legs.

crack *n.* A **crack** is a thin line where something is ready to break.
*We had to put in a new window because the old one had a **crack** in it.*

cracker *n.* A **cracker** is a thin, crisp baked snack.

crash *v. (crashes, crashing, crashed)* **Crash** means to smash into something else very hard.
*The plate **crashed** to the floor and broke into little pieces.*

crawl *v.* To **crawl** is to move on your hands and knees.
*Most babies **crawl** before they walk.*

crayon *n.* A **crayon** is a kind of wax pencil that comes in lots of colors. It is used for drawing or writing.

creature *n.* Any animal is a **creature**.
*Owls are creatures of the **night**.*

cross *v.* **Cross** means to go from one side to the other side.
*Dad says I may now **cross** the street by myself.*

crowd *n.* A **crowd** is a big group of people.

crown *n.* A **crown** is a kind of hat of gold and jewels worn by kings and queens.

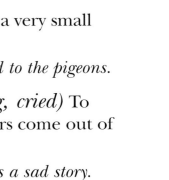

crumb *n.* A **crumb** is a very small piece of bread or cake.
*We fed the **crumbs** of bread to the pigeons.*

cry *v. (cries, crying, cried)* To **cry** means to have tears come out of your eyes.
*Sophia will **cry** if she hears a sad story.*

cube *n.* A **cube** is a solid shape made up of six equal square sides.

cup *n.* A **cup** is like a small bowl with a handle.

curl *n.* A **curl** is a piece of hair that curves.

curve *n.* A **curve** is a bend in a line or a road.

cut *v. (cuts, cutting, cut)* **Cut** means to make an opening in something with a sharp tool.
*Mom **cut** open the package with the scissors.*

A B C **D** E F G H I J K L M

Dd

dance *v.* *(dancing, dances, danced)* To **dance** means to move the body along with music.

danger *n.* **Danger** means being close to getting hurt.

*Climbing too high, Lisa was in **danger** of falling.*

dark *adj.* **Dark** means having no light.

date *n.* A **date** is the day, month, and year something happens.

*The **date** I was born was April 3, 1992.*

daughter *n.* A **daughter** is a girl child of a man and woman.

day *n.* *(days)* A **day** is 24 hours of time. A day begins at midnight and ends the following midnight.

deaf *adj.* **Deaf** means not able to hear any sounds.

decide *v.* **Decide** means to make up your mind.

*Sometimes it is hard to **decide** what I want for lunch.*

deep *adj.* **Deep** means going very far down.

*Jake used a shovel to dig a **deep** hole.*

delicious *adj.* **Delicious** means a food tastes very good.

desk *n.* A **desk** is a table that we do work on.

*Oscar does all his homework at his **desk**.*

deliver *v.* To **deliver** something means to bring it where it is supposed to go.

*The messenger **delivered** the package to our door.*

desert *n.* A **desert** is a place that is hot, dry, and sandy.

*The wind makes patterns in the **desert** sand.*

dessert *n.* **Dessert** is a food eaten at the end of a meal.

*After dinner, I had apple pie with strawberries for **dessert**.*

diamond *n.* A **diamond** is a hard, sparkling jewel that comes from inside the earth.

*She had a **diamond** ring.*

diary *n.* *(diaries)* A **diary** is a book where you write about what happens in your day.

dictionary *n.* *(dictionaries)* A **dictionary** is a book that lists words in alphabetical order and gives their meanings.

different *adj.* **Different** means not the same.

difficult *adj.*
Difficult means hard to do.
*At first writing was **difficult**, but now it is easy.*

dig *v. (digs, digging, dug)* **Dig** means to make a hole in the ground.

dinner *n.* **Dinner** is often the main meal of the day, and is eaten in the evening.
*Mom baked a turkey for **dinner**.*

dinosaur *n.* **Dinosaurs** were reptiles that lived millions of years ago.

direction *n.* **Direction** means the way you are going.
*When we got lost, we asked the policeman for **directions**.*

dirt *n.* **Dirt** is another word for soil or earth.

disappear *v.* **Disappear** is when something suddenly becomes invisible.
*The magician at Billy's party made the rabbit **disappear**.*

discover *v.* **Discover** means to find or learn something new.
*Annie **discovered** that a raccoon was living beneath the front steps.*

dish *n. (dishes)* A **dish** is a container for holding or serving food.

distance *n.* **Distance** is the space between two things or places.
*The **distance** from New York to Los Angeles is about 3,000 miles.*

disturb *v.* **Disturb** means to bother someone or something.
*Don't **disturb** Grandpa while he is taking his nap.*

dive *v. (diving, dived, dove)* **Dive** means to jump into deep water headfirst.
*I **dive** into the pool from the diving board.*

divide *v.* **Divide** means to separate something into pieces.
*We will **divide** the orange into slices.*

do *v. (does, doing, did)* **Do** means to make something happen.
*When will you **do** your homework?*

doll *n.* A **doll** is a toy that is shaped like a person.

door *n.* A **door** is an opening to a building or room that people use to come in or out.

double *adj.* Something is **double** when it is twice as much.
*I had two cards, but Bill had **double** with four.*

down *adj.*
Down means coming from a higher to a lower place.
*Come **down** the stairs and say hello to Grandma.*

dragon *n.* A **dragon** is a make-believe monster. It has wings, scaly skin, and can breathe fire out of its nose.

draw *v. (drawing, drew, drawn)* To **draw** means to make a picture with a pen, pencil, or crayon.

drawer *n.* A **drawer** is an open box for storing things. It slides in and out of a piece of furniture or a cabinet.
*My socks are in the second **drawer**.*

A B C **D** E F G H I J K L M

drawing *n.* A **drawing** is a picture made with a pencil, pen, or crayons.

drip *n.* A **drip** is when a liquid falls from something drop by drop.

*The kitchen sink had a bad **drip**.*

dream *n.* A **dream** is something you see and hear in your mind when you are asleep.

dress¹ *n.* (dresses) A **dress** is a piece of clothing that girls or women wear. It goes from the shoulders to below the waist.

dress² *v.*
To **dress** also means to put clothes on.

drink¹ *v.* (drinking, drank, drunk) **drink** means to swallow a liquid.

drink² *n.* A **drink** is also any liquid we swallow.

drive *v.* (driving, drove, driven) To **drive** means to steer a motor vehicle in the direction you want.

*Roy **drives** trucks and tractors on his farm.*

drop¹ *n.* A **drop** is a tiny bit of liquid.

drop² *v.* **Drop** also means to let something fall.

*If you **drop** that bottle, it will break.*

dry *adj.* (drier, driest)
Dry means not wet.

*Don't touch the paint until it is **dry**!*

dust *n.* **Dust** is many tiny pieces of dry dirt.

Ee

Earth *n.* **Earth** is the name of our planet.

earth *n.* **Earth** is also dirt or soil.

*Molly planted the flowers in the **earth**.*

east *n.* **East** is the direction where the sun comes up.

*The sun rises in the **east** and sets in the west.*

easy *adj.* (easier, easiest)
Easy means not difficult.

*Jeff thinks arithmetic is **easy** to do.*

eat *v.* (eating, ate, eaten) **Eat** means to chew and swallow food.

echo *n.* An **echo** is when you hear a sound twice because it bounces off something.

*We shouted into the cave to hear our **echo** come back.*

edge *n.* An **edge** is the part along the end or side of something.

*If the plate is too close to the **edge** of the table, it might fall off.*

egg *n.* An **egg** has a thin, hard shell to protect the babies of birds, fish, or reptiles that grow inside.

*Have you ever seen a chick hatch from an **egg**?*

empty *adj. (emptier, emptiest)* **Empty** means there is nothing inside.

end *n.* **End** means the last part or when something is finished.

energy *n.* To have **energy** is to feel strong and active.

*It takes a lot of **energy** to run fast.*

engine *n.* An **engine** is a motor that makes a machine go.

enough *adj.* **Enough** means to have as much as you need.

*Does the car have **enough** gas to get to the store?*

enter *v.* **Enter** means to go in.

*Please **enter** through the back door.*

envelope *n.* An **envelope** is a flat paper container for letters.

*The blue **envelope** is addressed to Kim.*

equal *adj.* **Equal** means the same amount.

*Four quarters are **equal** to one dollar.*

escape *v.* **Escape** means to get free.

*Peter Rabbit was able to **escape** from Mr. MacGregor's garden.*

even[1] *adj.* **Even** means that something is flat.

even[2] *adv.* **Even** also means equally divided.

evening *n.* **Evening** is the time of day just after the sun goes down.

*We are going to a movie this **evening**.*

every *adj.* **Every** means each one in a group.

***Every** student in my class has a desk.*

excellent *adj.* **Excellent** means very, very good.

excuse *n.* An **excuse** is a reason or explanation for something.

*Being sick was Tony's **excuse** for missing school.*

exercise *v.* To **exercise** means to move the body to make it strong and keep it healthy.

*Beth **exercises** by jogging twice a week.*

exit *n.* An **exit** is the way out of a place.

*Buildings always have signs above the **exits**.*

expensive *adj.* **Expensive** means costing a lot of money.

*The fancy car was too **expensive**, so we bought a cheaper one.*

$$3 \times 5 = 15$$
$$3 \times 6 = 18$$
$$3 \times 7 = 21$$

explain *v.* **Explain** is to tell about something so that others can understand it.

*The teacher will **explain** the lesson.*

explode *v.* **Explode** means something breaking up into lots of small pieces all at once.

On the Fourth of July, fireworks **explode** *across the sky.*

explore *v.* **Explore** means to find out all about something.

extra *adj.* **Extra** means more of something than is needed.

We took the **extra** *food home in a doggie bag.*

Ff

factory *n.* *(factories)* A **factory** is a building where people use machines to make things.

fair[1] *adj.* To be **fair** means to treat everyone equally.

To be **fair**, *everyone will get a turn to ride the pony.*

fair[2] *n.* A **fair** is also a place where people go to play games, go on rides, and where farmers sometimes show their best animals.

fairy *n.* *(fairies)* A **fairy** is a tiny make-believe creature that has magical powers.

fall *v.* *(falling, fell, fallen)* **Fall** means to drop suddenly to the ground.

Sometimes ripe apples **fall** *from the tree.*

false *adj.* **False** means not true.

The idea that the earth is flat is **false**.

family *n.* *(families)* A **family** is a group of people who are related to you or who care for you.

My grandparents, aunts, uncles, and cousins are all part of my **family**.

famous *adj.* **Famous** means a person, place, or thing that is well known.

The Statue of Liberty is a **famous** *landmark.*

far *adv.* *(farther, farthest)* **Far** means not close.

The sun is very **far** *from the earth.*

farm *n.* A **farm** is a place where animals are raised and crops are grown.

farm animals

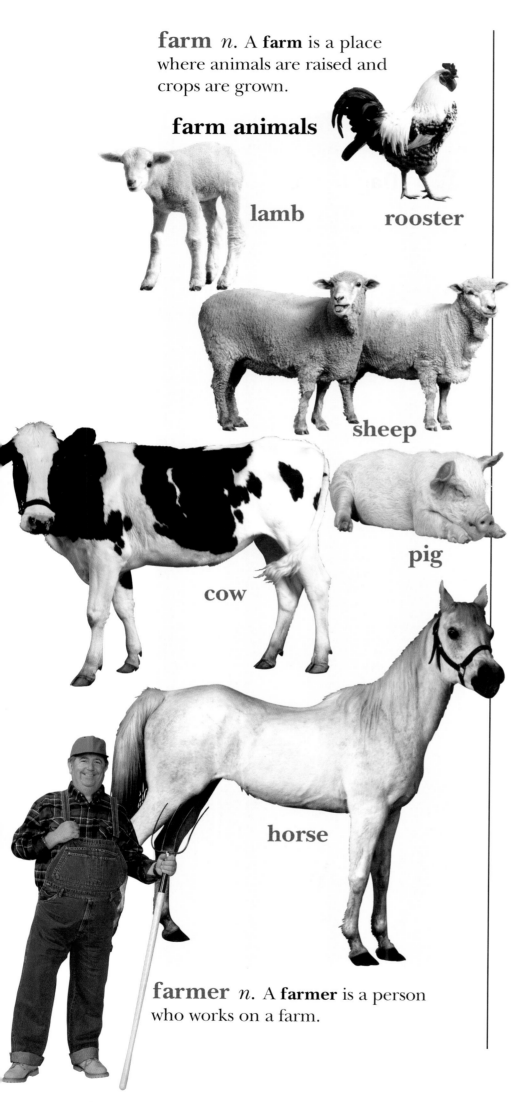

lamb

rooster

sheep

cow

pig

horse

farmer *n.* A **farmer** is a person who works on a farm.

fast *adj.* **Fast** means quick.

*The cars and trucks on the highway were going very **fast**.*

father *n.*
A **father** is the male parent.

favorite *n.*
A **favorite** is the one you like the best.

fear *n.* **Fear** means being scared.

feather *n.* **Feathers** cover a bird's body. They keep it warm and help the bird to fly.

feed *v.* (*feeding, fed*) **Feed** means to give food to a person or animal.

*It is Jerry's job to **feed** the cat.*

feel *v.* (*feeling, felt*) **Feel** means to touch.

*The bunnies' fur **feels** soft.*

female n. Animals and people are either **female** or male. Females are able to have babies. Girls and women are female.

*My mother and sister are **females**.*

fence *n.* A **fence** is something like a wall that is built outside. Fences are often made of wood, stone, or wire.

*Our **fence** keeps deer out of the flower garden.*

fever *n.* A **fever** means our body temperature is too hot.

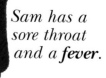

*Sam has a sore throat and a **fever**.*

A B C D E F G H I J K L M

few *adj.* **Few** means not many.

I can only stay for a few minutes.

field *n.* A **field** is a piece of land without trees or buildings.

The field next to our school is a clear place to play.

fill *v.* To **fill** is to put as much of something into a container as it will hold.

We filled the jar with jelly beans.

film *n.* **Film** is a thin piece of plastic we use to make photographs.

I don't have any pictures of the end of the game because I ran out of film.

find *v.* (finding, found) **Find** means to locate what you are looking for.

It took me an hour to find my sneakers.

finish *v.* (finishes, finishing, finished) **Finish** means to end.

When you finish the test, raise your hand.

fire *n.* A **fire** is the light, flame, and heat that come from something burning.

At camp, we built a fire so that we could stay warm.

first *adj.* **First** means the one before any others.

Bob was the first one on the team to shoot a basket.

fish/fisherman *n.* (fishes) **Fish** live in the water. They have fins, scales, a tail and breathe air through an opening called gills.

A **fisherman** is someone who catches fish.

fit *v.* (fits, fitting, fitted) **Fit** means to be the right size.

These shoes don't fit me anymore.

fix *v.* (fixes, fixed) **Fix** means to repair something.

flag *n.* A **flag** is a piece of cloth with different shapes and colors on it.

Each star on the flag of the United States stands for one of the 50 states.

flame *n.* **Flames** are the hot, bright lights that are part of a fire.

flat *adj.* **Flat** means having no bumps or holes.

The workers filled in the holes in the road to make it flat.

flash *n.* A **flash** is a short and sudden burst of light.

The flash of lightning lit up the whole forest.

flavor *n.* A **flavor** is what something tastes like.

This drink has a lemon flavor.

float *v.* To **float** means to stay on top of the water or up in the air.

A feather can float in the air.

flood *n.* A **flood** is when too much water covers an area that is supposed to be dry.

The sink overflowed and made a flood in the bathroom.

floor *n.* A **floor** is the part of a room that you stand on.

flour *n.* **Flour** is a powder made from grains like wheat.

Flour is used to make bread, cakes, and other foods.

N O P Q R S T U V W X Y Z

flower *n.* A **flower** is the part of the plant that makes seeds, fruit, and blossoms.

carnation

daisy

gladiola

daffodil

lily

tulip

sunflower

rose

fly *v. (flies, flying, flew, flown)* **Fly** means to move through the air.

*Most birds can **fly**, but ostriches and penguins cannot.*

fold *v.* **Fold** means to bend one part of something over on itself.

*I **fold** my sweater before putting it in the drawer.*

follow *v.* **Follow** means to go behind.

food *n.* **Food** is what we eat, such as bread, fruit, cheese, meat, and vegetables.

forest *n.* A **forest** is a large area of land covered with trees.

forget *v. (forgetting, forgot, forgotten)* To **forget** means you do not remember.

*Did you **forget** to take your milk money to school today?*

forgive *v. (forgiving, forgave, forgiven)* **Forgive** is to stop feeling angry at someone who has hurt you.

*Please **forgive** me for forgetting to invite you to my party.*

fork *n.* A **fork** is a tool used for eating. It has a handle and sharp points at the end for sticking into food.

forward *adv.* **Forward** is the direction in front of you.

*We all walked **forward** to get off the bus.*

frame *n.* A **frame** is the edge around something. It often is made of wood or metal.

*My mother has a picture of me in a **frame** on her desk.*

A B C D E F G H I J K L M

free¹ *adj.* **Free** means able to come and go without being stopped.

*The cage was opened and the bird was set **free**.*

free² *adj.* **Free** also means not costing any money.

freeze *v. (freezing, froze, frozen)* **Freeze** means to change from liquid to solid.

*When the pond **freezes**, we can skate on it.*

fresh *adj.* **Fresh** means just made.

*Would you like some **fresh** orange juice?*

friend *n.* A **friend** is someone you know well and like to do things with.

*I walk to school every day with my best **friend**.*

frighten *v.* **Frighten** means to scare.

front *n.* **Front** is the other side of the back.

*The mailbox is at the **front** of our house.*

frown *v.* A **frown** is a sad face made by turning down the corners of the mouth.

*The baby will **frown** if you take her bottle away.*

frost *n.* **Frost** is a thin layer of ice that you cannot see through.

frozen *adj.* **Frozen** is when things become hard from the cold.

*The water in the bucket in our backyard became **frozen** overnight.*

fruit *n.* The **fruit** is the part of the plant that holds the seeds. It is also good to eat.

*Some **fruit** has to be peeled before eating it.*

apple

bananas

blueberries

cantaloupe

grapes

kiwis

lemon

lime

orange

pineapple

tomato

strawberries

N O P Q R S T U V Y

fry *v. (fries, frying, fried)* **Fry** means to cook something in hot fat or oil.

full *adj.* **Full** means that there is no room left.

*The cup on my Mom's desk is **full** of pens and pencils.*

fun *n.* **Fun** means to have a good time.

funny *adj. (funnier, funniest)* **Funny** is something that makes you laugh.

*Vinny's joke was so **funny** I couldn't stop laughing.*

fur *n.* **Fur** is the soft coat of hair covering an animal's body.

furry *adj.* We say something that has fur is **furry**.

*That bear is really **furry**.*

furnace *n.* A **furnace** is a large machine that makes heat.

*The repairman is in the basement fixing the **furnace**.*

furniture *n.* **Furniture** is things like tables, chairs, and beds that you use in a house.

*When we moved to our new house, all our **furniture** filled a big truck.*

future *n.* The **future** is the time that has not happened yet.

*I will attend college in the **future**.*

Gg

game *n.* A **game** is an activity with special rules that is played for fun.

*Let's play a **game** of hide-and-seek.*

garage *n.* A **garage** is a building where cars are kept.

garden *n.* A **garden** is a piece of land near a house where flowers or vegetables are grown.

Julie takes flowers from her garden.

gas¹ *n. (gases)* **Gas** is a liquid made from oil that makes cars and other machines go.

*We need to fill the car with **gas** before our trip.*

gas² *n.* **Gas** is also something that is not a solid or a liquid, like air.

gentle *adj.* **Gentle** means being kind and careful.

*Ted is always **gentle** with the baby.*

giant *n.* A **giant** is a very big, strong person you read about in fairy tales.

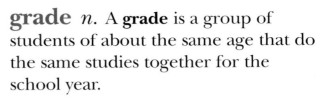

girl *n.* A **girl** is a female child.

give *v.* *(giving, gave, given)* To **give** means to let another person have something.
*Please **give** me a new pencil.*

glad *adj.* **Glad** means happy.
*I'm **glad** we are going to the party.*

glasses *n.* **Glasses** are lenses in frames worn over the eyes to help people see better.
*I can see the words on the blackboard when I wear my **glasses**.*

glass *n.* *(glasses)* **Glass** is a smooth, breakable material you can see through.
*Our school nurse keeps cotton balls in a **glass** container.*

globe *n.* A **globe** is a round shape with a map of the Earth shown on it.
*Can you find the United States on the **globe**?*

glue *n.* **Glue** is a liquid that makes things stick together.

go *v.* *(goes, going, went)* **Go** means to move from one place to another.
*The green light means "**go!**"*

gold *n.* **Gold** is a valuable yellow metal found in rocks. It is used to make jewelry and coins.

good *adj.* **Good** means something you like.

goodbye *n.* **Goodbye** is a word people say when they leave each other.
*I say **goodbye** to my mother each day when I leave for school.*

grade *n.* A **grade** is a group of students of about the same age that do the same studies together for the school year.
*Next year I'll be six and will be in the first **grade**.*

grain *n.* **Grain** is the seed of a cereal grass, such as wheat, oats, and rice.
*Oatmeal is made from the **grain** of oats.*

grandfather *n.* A **grandfather** is the father of one of your parents.
*Some people call their **grandfathers** grandpa or granddad.*

grandmother *n.* A **grandmother** is the mother of one of your parents.
*Some people call their **grandmothers** grandma or granny.*

grass *n.* *(grasses)* **Grass** is a plant with thin green leaves that grows in fields, parks, and yards.

great¹ *adj.* **Great** means very big or important.
*The **Great** Wall of China is a stone fence that is hundreds of miles long.*

great² *adj.* **Great** also means very good.

ground *n.* The **ground** is the land you walk on.
*The **ground** is muddy after a hard rain.*

group *n.* A **group** is three or more people or things together.
*We stood in a **group** for the picture.*

grow *v. (growing, grew, grown)*
Grow means to get bigger.
*The seedling will **grow** into a tree.*

growl *v.*
To **growl** is to make an angry sound.
*My dog will **growl** at strangers.*

guard[1] *n.*
A **guard** is a person whose job is to keep people or things safe.
*Mr. Jones is a crossing **guard**.*

guard[2] *v.* **Guard** also means to watch people or things.
*Mr. Jones **guards** the bank during the night.*

guess *v. (guesses, guessing, guessed)* **Guess** means to give an answer even if you are not sure it is correct.
*Can you **guess** how many jelly beans are in this jar?*

gym *n.* A **gym** is a place where people exercise and play sports.

gymnastics *n.* **Gymnastics** is a sport where you stretch, turn, roll, tumble, and jump.

Hh

half *n. (halves)*
Half means one of two equal parts.
*We cut the melon in **half**.*

hammer *n.* A **hammer** is a tool with a handle and a heavy metal piece at one end. It is used to hit nails.

handle *n.* A **handle** is the part of a an object you hold.

hang *v. (hanging, hanged, hung)* **Hang** means to attach something from its top.
*I **hang** our clothes on the wire.*

happy *adj. (happier, happiest)*
Happy means to feel joy.

hard[1] *adj.* **Hard** means solid and not easy to break.
*Steel is a **hard** metal.*

hard[2] *adv.*
Hard also means difficult.
*This puzzle is **hard** to do.*

have *v.* To **have** something is to hold it or **have** it be a part of you.

*I **have** blue eyes.*

healthy *adj. (healthier, healthiest)* **Healthy** means you are not sick.

*Tami plays lots of sports and is very **healthy**.*

hear *v. (hears, hearing, heard)* **Hear** is to use your ears to notice sounds.

*Can you **hear** the music?*

heart *n.* The **heart** is a muscle in your chest that pumps blood through the body.

heat *n.*

Heat is what makes us feel warm.

*For **heat**, we built a fire in the fireplace.*

heavy *adj. (heavier, heaviest)* **Heavy** means something weighs a lot.

*The weights are very **heavy**.*

helicopter *n.*

A **helicopter** is a flying machine with a propeller on top.

***Helicopters** can fly straight up and down.*

help *v.* **Help** is to do something useful for someone.

*Kate **helps** Mary with her homework.*

here *adv.*

Here means at a certain place.

*José wants to eat lunch **here**, but I want to eat in the backyard.*

hero/heroine *n.* A **hero** is a boy or man who does a brave thing for someone else.

A **heroine** is a girl or woman who does a brave thing for someone else.

hide *v. (hiding, hid, hidden)* To **hide** is to put something where it will be hard to find.

*When we play hide-and-seek, I like to **hide** in the closet.*

high *adj.* **High** means far above the ground.

*We were as **high** as you could climb.*

hill *n.* A **hill** is land that is higher than the ground around it.

*We climbed to the top of the **hill**.*

hit *v. (hits, hitting, hit)* If you **hit** something, you swing hard at it.

*I **hit** the ball with the tennis racquet.*

hold *n. (holds, holding, held)* **Hold** means to have something in your hands or arms.

*Ben **held** the ball against his leg.*

hole *n.*

A **hole** is an opening.

*The ball stopped at the very edge of the **hole**.*

home *n.* **Home** is a place where people or animals live.

*This nest is a bird's **home**.*

honest *adj.*

Honest means telling the truth.

*An **honest** person can be trusted.*

honey *n.* **Honey** is a sweet, sticky food made by bees.

hope *v. (hopes, hoping, hoped)* **Hope** means to believe that something you want will happen.

I hope it will be sunny when we go to the beach.

hospital *n.* A **hospital** is a building where doctors and nurses take care of sick or injured people.

Megan went to the hospital when she broke her finger.

hot *adj. (hotter, hottest)* **Hot** means having a high temperature.

Be careful, the stove is very hot!

hour *n.* An **hour** is an amount of time equal to 60 minutes.

how *adv.* **How** means in what way.

How does a computer work?

hug *v. (hugged)* **Hug** means to hold someone or something tightly in your arms.

Uncle Bob hugs me when he sees me.

human *n.* A **human** is a person.

hungry *adj. (hungrier, hungriest)* **Hungry** means wanting to eat.

Jake is always hungry after school.

hurry *v. (hurries, hurrying, hurried)* **Hurry** means to move quickly.

Hurry, or we will miss the bus!

hurt *v. (hurts, hurting, hurt)* To **hurt** is to cause pain or harm.

George hurt his arm when he fell off his bike.

husband *n.* A **husband** is a married man.

Frank is Sally's husband.

Ii

ice *n.* **Ice** is frozen water.

ice cream *n.* **Ice cream** is a sweet frozen food that comes in many flavors.

ice skate *n.* An **ice skate** is a boot with a metal blade on the bottom that lets us move across ice very fast.

idea *n.* An **idea** is something you think of.

It was my idea to have pizza for dinner.

ill *adj.* Being **ill** means being sick.

I felt very ill on the boat trip.

imagine *v.* **Imagine** means to have a picture of something in your head.

*I like to **imagine** that I am a ballerina.*

immediately *adv.* **Immediately** means something happens right away.

*We have to get on the bus **immediately**.*

important *adj.* **Importan**t means something that matters very much.

*It is **important** to drink clean water.*

impossible *adj.* **Impossible** means not able to happen.

*It is **impossible** to walk on your nose.*

inch *n. (inches)*
An **inch** is a measurement.

***Inches** are marked on a ruler.*

information *n.* **Information** is facts that tell you about a subject.

initial *n.* An **initial** is the first letter of a name or a word.

*Robert Williams has the **initials** R.W.*

ink *n.* **Ink** is the colored liquid that pens use for writing.

*The teacher corrected the tests using a pen with red **ink**.*

insect *n.* An **insect** is a small animal with a head, chest, stomach, and six legs.

*Dragonflies and ladybugs are **insects**.*

inside *adj.* To be **inside** is the opposite of outside.

*Terry played **inside** and Maria played outside.*

instructions *n.* **Instructions** are what tell us how to do something.

instrument *n.* An **instrument** is something you play to make music.

insects

ant

bee

beetle

butterfly

cricket

fly

ladybug

moth

wasp

N O P Q R S T U V W X Y Z

interesting *adj.* **Interesting** means something that you enjoy learning about.
*Emily thinks dinosaurs are **interesting**.*

interrupt *v.* **Interrupt** means to stop someone from what they are saying or doing.
*Don't **interrupt** Mom while she is talking.*

invent *v.* **Invent** means to make something for the first time.

invention *n.* An **invention** is something that has been thought of or has been made for the first time.
*The internet is an **invention** that has changed the world.*

investigate *v.* When you **investigate** something, you find out all you can about it.
*We wanted to **investigate** the old barn to find out what was inside.*

invisible *adj.* **Invisible** means cannot be seen.
*Air is **invisible**.*

invite *v.* **Invite** means to ask someone to join you.
*Carl will **invite** all his friends to the party.*

iron¹ *n.* An **iron** is a tool with a flat metal bottom that is heated and used to press clothes.

iron² *n.* **Iron** is also a strong, dark metal dug from the ground.

island *n.* An **island** is land surrounded on all sides by water.

itch *n.* When you have an **itch**, you want to scratch your skin.
*My mosquito bites really made me **itch**.*

Jj

jam *n.* **Jam** is a thick, sweet food made from cooked fruit.

jar *n.* A **jar** is a glass container with a removable lid.

jelly *n.* *(jellies)* **Jelly** is made from fruit juice and sugar.
*Ethan had a peanut butter and **jelly** sandwich as a snack.*

jewelry *n.* **Jewelry** is removable decorations for the body.
*Rings, earrings, necklaces, and bracelets are **jewelry**.*

job *n.* A **job** is work that people are paid for doing.
*My summer **job** was cutting grass.*

join *v.* **Join** means to become part of a group.
*Would you like to **join** the soccer team?*

joke *n.* A **joke** is something that makes people laugh.

jobs

business person

dancer

cowboy

doctor

engineer

lawyer

fireman

musician

teacher

Kk

juice *n.* **Juice** is the liquid squeezed from fruits and vegetables.

jump *v.* **Jump** means to lift both feet off the ground at the same time.

*In hopscotch, we **jump** from square to square.*

jungle *n.* A **jungle** is a hot, damp place full of tall trees, plants, insects, and wild animals.

just *adv.* **Just** means a small amount.

*Please give me **just** a little more salad.*

keep[1] *v. (keeps, keeping, kept)* **Keep** means to hold on to something.

*I'm going to **keep** this silver dollar instead of spending it.*

keep[2] *v.* **Keep** also means to put something in a certain place.

*I **keep** the umbrella in the hall closet.*

key *n.* A **key** is a tool that opens a lock.

kick *v.* **Kick** means to hit something with the foot.

*Gary **kicked** the soccer ball to Joan.*

kind[1] *adj.* **Kind** means being helpful to others.

*It was **kind** of you to help Mr. Henson shovel the snow on his driveway.*

kind[2] *n.* **Kind** also means a group of things that are alike.

*A plum is a **kind** of fruit.*

king *n.* A **king** is a man who rules a country.

***King** Arthur ruled over his kingdom.*

kiss *v.* **Kiss** means to touch another person with your lips.

kit *n.* A **kit** is a collection of things used to build or make something.

*Alvin received the model robot **kit** he wanted for his birthday*

kitchen *n.* A **kitchen** is a room where food is prepared.

kite *n.* A **kite** is a toy that flies through the air while attached to a ball of string.

*My **kite** is made of paper and looks like a dragon.*

kneel *v. (kneels, kneeling, knelt)* **Kneel** means to get down on your knees.

*You have to **kneel** to look under the bed.*

knife *n. (knives)* A **knife** is a sharp tool for cutting things.

*I use a **knife** to cut meat.*

knight *n.* A **knight** was a soldier from long ago who fought for his king or queen.

*In many fairy tales, a **knight** goes on a journey to do a good deed.*

knock *v.* **Knock** means to tap on something with the knuckles of your hand.

***Knock** on the door to see if anyone is home.*

knot *n.* A **knot** is the twisted part where something has been tied.

*I tie a **knot** on the end of the thread before I begin to sew.*

know *v. (knows, knowing, knew, known)* **Know** means to have learned and remembered something.

*I **know** my multiplication tables.*

Ll

ladder *n.* A **ladder** is a set of steps used to reach high places.

*Dad climbed the **ladder** to the roof.*

lake *n.* A **lake** is a body of water surrounded by land.

*We rowed our boat all the way across the **lake** and back.*

lamp *n.* A **lamp** gives off light using electricity or fire.

*I turn on the **lamp** when I want to read.*

land[1] *n.* The **land** is the ground we walk on.

land[2] *v.* **Land** means to come from the sky to the ground.

*The plane will **land** in one hour.*

language *n.* A **language** is all the words we use to speak and write.

lap *n.* When someone is sitting down, their **lap** is the part on top of their legs.

*I sat on Grandpa's **lap** while he read me a story.*

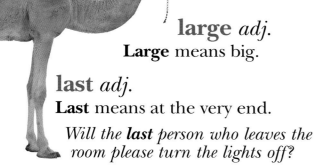

large *adj.*
Large means big.

last *adj.*
Last means at the very end.

*Will the **last** person who leaves the room please turn the lights off?*

late *adj.* **Late** means arriving after the expected time.

*We waited a long time because the bus was **late**.*

laugh *v.* To **laugh** is to make the sounds that show you think something is funny.

*Tommy tells jokes that make me **laugh**.*

lay *v. (lays, laying, laid)* **Lay** means to put something down carefully.

*Please **lay** your books on the table.*

lazy *adj. (lazier, laziest)*
Lazy means not wanting to do anything.

*Hot weather makes our dog feel **lazy**.*

lead *v.*
(lead, leading, led)
Lead means to go first.

*Robert, will you **lead** the class to the cafeteria?*

leader *n.* A **leader** is someone who sets an example of how to act.

leaf *n. (leaves)* A **leaf** is the flat, green part of a plant that grows from the stem or from a branch.

lean¹ *v.* **Lean** means to bend in the direction of something.

*Billy **leaned** on the desk.*

lean² *adj.* **Lean** also means thin or having little fat.

learn *v.* **Learn** means to get to know about something.

*My little brother will **learn** how to ride a bicycle this year.*

leather *n.*
Leather is the dried skin of an animal.

*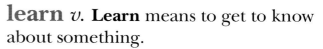**Leather** is used to make clothes, furniture, and other things.*

leave *v. (leaves, leaving, left)*
Leave means to go away from a place.

*I **leave** home every morning at 7:30 to go to school.*

left *n.* **Left** is the opposite of right.

*We begin reading on the **left** side of the page.*

length *n.* Something's **length** is how long it is.

less *adv.*
Less means not as much.

*Megan's glass holds much **less** milk than Beth's glass.*

lesson *n.* A **lesson** is a time set aside to learn something.

*I have a piano **lesson** for one hour every Monday.*

letter¹ *n.* A **letter** is one of the 26 signs that make up the alphabet.

*"A" is the first **letter** of the alphabet.*

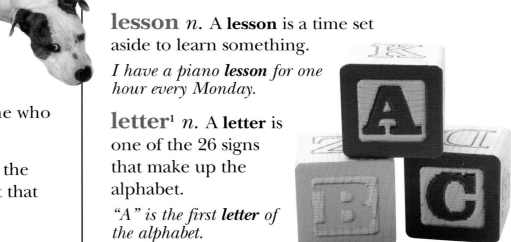

letter² *n.* A **letter** is also a message sent in the mail.

*I wrote a **letter** to my grandmother to thank her for my present.*

library *n. (libraries)* A **library** is a place people can go to read or borrow books.

lick *v.* **Lick** means to move your tongue over something.

*A lollipop lasts longer if you **lick** it and don't bite it.*

lie¹ *v. (lying, lay, lain)* **Lie** means to have your body in a flat position.

*We like to **lie** on the floor when we watch TV.*

lie² *v. (lie, lying, lied)* To tell a **lie** is to say something that is not true.

life *n. (lives)* **Life** means the time something is alive.

lift *v.* **Lift** means to pick something up.

light¹ *n.* **Light** is what we need to be able to see.

***Light** comes from the Sun.*

light² *v. (light, lighting, lit)*

To **light** is to make something bright or start to burn.

*When the electric lights go out, we **light** candles.*

light³ *adj.* **Light** means a color that is not dark.

*Yellow is a very **light** color.*

light⁴ *adj.* **Light** also means not heavy.

*The pillow is **light**.*

lightning *n.*

Lightning is a bright flash in the sky during a storm.

like¹ *v. (like, liked, liking)*

Like means to have good feelings about someone or something.

*Duane **likes** to play at Carla's house.*

like² *adj.* **Like** also means similar to something else.

*Her shoes are **like** mine.*

line *n.* A **line** is a long mark.

*We used a ruler to draw straight **lines**.*

A **line** is also a row of people or things.

*I had to stand in **line** to buy my lunch.*

liquid *n.* **Liquid** is something wet that can be poured.

*Some medicines can be taken both as a pill or a **liquid**.*

list *n.* A **list** is a group of words with a purpose.

*Mom had a **list** of things to buy at the grocery store.*

listen *v.* To **listen** means to try to hear.

*If you **listen** carefully, you can hear the birds singing.*

little *adj.* **Little** means small.

live *v.* To **live** is to be alive and full of life.

*Our dog **lived** a long time.*

To **live** somewhere means that is where your home is.

*Pierre **lives** on Temple Street.*

lock¹ *n.* A **lock** keeps things from being opened.

*I have a small **lock** on my diary.*

lock² *v.* To **lock** is to close with a key.

*Please **lock** the front door.*

lonely *adj. (lonelier, loneliest)*

Lonely means feeling sad because you are alone.

*I was **lonely** while my brother was away at camp last summer.*

A B C D E F G H I J K **L M**

long *adj.* If something is **long**, there's a big distance from one end of it to the other.

*The bird's feathers are **long**.*

look *v.* To **look** means to use your eyes to see.

***Look** at the computer screen!*

loose¹ *adj.* **Loose** means not tied up or locked in.

*How did the parrot get **loose**?*

loose² *adj.* **Loose** also means not tight.

*My brother's jacket is **loose** on me.*

lose¹ *v. (lose, losing, lost)* **Lose** means not able to find something.

*If you **lose** your pencil, you will have nothing to write with.*

lose² *v.* To **lose** also means to not win.

lost¹ *adj.* **Lost** means that something cannot be found.

*My keys are **lost**.*

lost² *adj.* **Lost** also means not knowing where you are.

*On the first day of school, I got **lost** in the hall.*

loud *adj.* **Loud** means a sound that can be heard from far away.

love *v.* **Love** is when you like someone very, very much.

*Grandma **loves** grandpa.*

low *adj.* **Low** means near the ground.

*The wall was **low** enough to jump over.*

lunch *n. (lunches)* **Lunch** is the meal between breakfast and dinner.

Mm

machine *n.* A **machine** is something people use to make work easier.

*A lawnmower is a handy **machine** used for cutting grass.*

magic *n.* **Magic** makes something that is impossible look like it is real.

magician *n.* A **magician** is a person who does magic tricks.

main *adj.* **Main** means the most important.

*The **main** ingredients for the cake are flour, sugar, and eggs.*

make *v. (makes, making, made)* **Make** means to build something or put it together.

*Let's **make** breakfast for Mom and Dad.*

male *n.* Animals and people are either **male** or female. Males cannot have babies. Boys and men are males.

N O P Q R S T U V W X Y Z

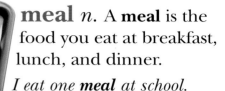

mammal *n.* A **mammal** is any animal that drinks milk from its mother when it is a baby.

Both cows and people are **mammals**.

man *n. (men)* A **man** is a grown-up person.

many *adj.* **Many** means lots.

There are **many** *berries in the bowl.*

map *n.* **Maps** are drawings that show us where we are.

We followed the **map** *to find the new camp.*

mask *n.* A **mask** is something worn to hide or protect the face.

I wear my catcher's **mask** *when I play baseball.*

match¹ *n. (matches)* A **match** is a thin piece of wood or paper with a special tip that is used to start a fire.

match² *v.* **Match** means to go together.

This brown shirt and these brown shoes **match**.

material *n.* **Material** is what something is made of.

The tablecloth was made from a soft **material**.

matter *v.* To **matter** is to be important or to make a difference.

It **matters** *whether you brush your teeth or you do not.*

mattress *n. (mattresses)* A **mattress** is the soft part of the bed you sleep on.

meal *n.* A **meal** is the food you eat at breakfast, lunch, and dinner.

I eat one **meal** *at school.*

mean¹ *v.* If you know what something **means**, you understand it.

I know what that word **means**.

mean² *adj.* A **mean** person is not nice.

The Wicked Witch of the West in The Wizard of Oz *is* **mean**.

measure *v. (measuring)* To **measure** is to use a tool to find out the size of something.

I need to **measure** *the paper with a ruler before cutting it.*

meat *n.* **Meat** is the parts of an animal used as food.

medicine *n.* **Medicine** is something people take to make them better when they are sick.

meet *v. (meets, meeting, met)* **Meet** means to come together.

My big sister's band **meets** *every Monday to practice.*

melt *v.* **Melt** means to change from a solid to a liquid.

The ice in my drink is **melting**.

mess *n. (messes)* A **mess** is something that is not clean or neat.

My mother says my room is a **mess**.

metal *n.* **Metal** is a hard material that comes from the ground.

Gold and iron are **metals**.

microphone *n.* A **microphone** is an instrument that records sounds or makes them louder.

The singer used a microphone so she could be heard.

middle *adj.* **Middle** means the center of something.

The doughnuts have a hole in the middle.

milk *n.* **Milk** is a white liquid food that is made by female mammals.

People drink milk from cows.

mind *n.* The **mind** is the part of us that we use for thinking, feeling, and dreaming.

mine *pron.*

Mine means belonging to me.

The bicycle with the red stripe is mine.

minus *prep.* **Minus** means to subtract or take away

Three minus one equals two.

minute *n.*

A **minute** is 60 seconds of time.

mirror *n.* A **mirror** is a special kind of glass that shows what you look like.

miss[1] *v. (misses, missing, missed)* To **miss** means to fail to catch or to reach something.

I missed the ball that Kylie threw.

miss[2] *v.* **Miss** also means to feel sad because someone you like is not with you.

My cousin Eddie moved away and I miss him very much.

mistake *n.* A **mistake** is something that is not correct.

It was a mistake to turn right.

mix *v. (mixes)* **Mix** means to combine two or more things.

The chef mixed the cake batter.

model *n.* A **model** is a copy of something, usually smaller than what it is copied from.

I play with model cars and trucks all the time.

money *n.* **Money** is what you use to buy things.

monster *n.* A **monster** is a scary make-believe person or animal.

month *n.* A **month** is one of twelve periods of time that make up a year.

moon *n.* The **moon** is a body in space that moves around a planet.

mop *n.* A **mop** is a tool for washing floors. It has a long handle and strings of cloth at the end.

more *adj.* **More** means a larger or greater amount.

Five lemons are more than three lemons.

morning *n.* **Morning** is the time of day from midnight until noon.

most[1] *adj.* **Most** means almost all.

Most students my age can read.

most[2] *adj.* **Most** also means the biggest number or amount.

Bill collected the most candy last Halloween.

mother *n.*

A **mother** is the female parent.

N O P Q R S T U V W X Y Z

motor *n.* A **motor** is a machine that turns and makes things work.

Dad fixed the motor on the lawnmower.

motorcycle *n.* A **motorcycle** is like a big bicycle that has an engine to make it run.

mountain *n.* A **mountain** is rocky land that is much higher than a hill.

move¹ *v.* **Move** means to go from one place to another.

I moved my bicycle from the driveway into the garage.

move² *v.* **Move** also means to change where you live.

Last year, we moved to a house where my brother and I have our own rooms.

movie *n.* A **movie** is a show where people act out a story in front of cameras. We watch movies in theaters and on television.

I like the movies on the big screens in the theaters better than the movies on TV.

mud *n.* **Mud** is what we call dirt when it is wet and thick.

When it rains our mom makes us take our shoes off when we come in so we don't get mud in the house.

multiply *v. (multiplies)* **Multiply** means to add a number to itself a number of times.

To multiply four times three is adding 4 three times.

muscle *n.* **Muscles** are parts of the body that help you move.

museum *n.* A **museum** is a building where interesting things are kept for people to look at.

music/musician *n.* **Music** is a set of beautiful sounds made by instruments or the voice.

A **musician** is a person who plays music.

musical instruments

accordion

cello

flute

guitar

french horn

violin

piano

trumpet

mustache *n.* A **mustache** is hair that grows between the nose and mouth.

mystery *n. (mysteries)* A **mystery** is something that cannot be explained.

A B C D E F G H I J K L M

Nn

nail *n.* A **nail** is a thin piece of metal with a point at one end and a flat head at the other.

Nails are used to join pieces of wood together.

name *n.* A **name** is the word that a person or thing is known as.

*My brother's **name** is Michael.*

nature *n.* **Nature** is everything in the world except for things made by people.

*Trees, rivers, weather, and animals are all parts of **nature**.*

near *adv.* **Near** means close to.

*The dolls are **near** one another.*

neat *adj.* When things are **neat** they are where they are supposed to be.

*We put away all the dishes so the kitchen would be **neat**.*

necklace *n.* A **necklace** is jewelry you wear around your neck.

need *v.* When you **need** something, you have to have it.

*People **need** food and water.*

needle *n.* A **needle** is a tool for sewing made from a thin piece of metal with a point at one end and a hole at the other for thread.

neighbor *n.* A **neighbor** is a person who lives near you.

nest *n.* A **nest** is a home birds make for themselves and their babies.

never *adv.* **Never** means at no time.

new *adj.* **New** means just made.

news *n.* **News** is information about what has just happened.

next[1] *adj.* **Next** means the one right after.

*Vin is first in line, and I am **next**.*

next[2] *adj.* **Next** also means the one closest to.

*Bobby is standing **next** to his dog.*

nice[1] *adj.* **Nice** means friendly.

nice[2] *adj.* **Nice** also means good.

*My dog Scamp is **nice**.*

night *n.* **Night** is the time after the sun goes down.

N O P Q R S T U V W X Y Z

no[1] *adv.* **No** is the opposite of yes.

no[2] *adj.* **No** also means not one, none. *We have **no** apples in the refrigerator.*

nobody *pron.*
Nobody means not one person.
Nobody came to the yard sale because it rained all afternoon.

noise *n.* A **noise** is a sound.

none *pron.*
None means not even one.
*I needed a red crayon but there were **none** left in the box.*

noodle *n.* **Noodles** are a kind of pasta used in soups and baked dishes.
*Grandma showed us how to place the **noodles** when making lasagna.*

north *n.* **North** is a direction. If you face where the Sun comes up, north is on your left. It is the opposite of south.
*A compass needle always points to the **north**.*

nothing *pron.*
Nothing means not even one thing.
*Mom, I'm bored because there is **nothing** to do.*

now *adv.*
Now means at this moment.

nowhere *adv.* **Nowhere** means not any place.

number *n.* A **number** is what we use to count.

nut *n.* A **nut** is the fruit of a tree inside a hard shell.
*Almonds are my favorite kind of **nut**.*

Oo

ocean *n.* An **ocean** is one of the large bodies of salt water that covers most of the earth.
*The five **oceans** of the world are the Atlantic, Pacific, Indian, Antarctic, and Arctic.*

octopus *n.*
(octopuses) An **octopus** is a sea animal with eight long arms.

off *adv.* **Off** is the opposite of on.
*I turn **off** the lights when I leave the room.*

offer *v.* When you **offer** something to someone, you ask if they would like to have it.
*Aunt Mae **offered** us fresh cookies.*

office *n.* An **office** is a building where people do their jobs.

often *adv.* **Often** means happening many times.

oil *n.* **Oil** is a thick, slippery liquid.

*Some **oil** comes from plants and is used for cooking.*

old *adj.* **Old** means having lived a long time.

once *adv.* **Once** means one time.

only *adj.* **Only** means just one.

*The **only** teacher with red hair is Mr. Keith.*

open *v.* When something is **open**, it is not closed and you can go through it.

*Please **open** the door so Ross can come in.*

opposite[1] *n.* An **opposite** is when something is completely different from another.

*The **opposite** of cold is hot.*

opposite[2] *prep.* **Opposite** also means across from.

*Molly stood **opposite** her mother.*

orchestra *n.* An **orchestra** is a large group of people who play musical instruments together.

other[1] *adj.* **Other** means a different person or thing.

*I have to wear this hat because I lost my **other** one.*

other[2] *adj.* **Other** also means more.

*Do you have any **other** toys under your bed?*

oven *n.* An **oven** is a machine used for cooking or heating food.

own *v.* **Own** means to have something that is yours.

*I **own** a bicycle.*

Pp

page *n.* A **page** is a piece of paper in a book.

pain *n.* A **pain** is the feeling in the body when something hurts.

*When I stubbed my toe, I cried from the **pain**.*

paint[1] *n.* **Paint** is a liquid used to make pictures or to cover things with color.

paint[2] *v.* To **paint** also means putting paint on something.

painting *n.* A **painting** is a picture made with paint and a brush.

pair *n.* A **pair** means two things that go together.

*I am wearing my new **pair** of shoes.*

paper *n.* **Paper** is a material used to write on and make books out of.

parent *n.*
A **parent** is a mother or father.

park *n.* A **park** is an outdoor place where people go to relax and play.
*We went to the **park** for a picnic.*

part *n.*
A **part** is one piece of something.
*My leg is **part** of my whole body.*

party *n.* *(parties)* A **party** is when people get together on a special day to have fun.

pass *v.* *(pass, passing, passed)*
Pass means to go by without stopping.
*I **pass** the bank on the way to the bakery.*

past *n.*
The **past** is all the time before now.

paste *n.* **Paste** is a soft, thick material used to stick things together.

paw *n.* A **paw** is an animal's foot.

pay *v.* *(pays, paying, paid)* **Pay** means to give money to buy something.
*Diane must **pay** for the toy before she takes it out of the store.*

peace *n.* **Peace** is a time when things are quiet and safe.

pen *n.*
A **pen** is a tool for writing with ink.

pencil *n.* A **pencil** is a writing tool made of wood and lead.

penguin *n.* A **penguin** is a black-and-white bird with webbed feet and flippers instead of wings.
***Penguins** are birds but they cannot fly.*

person *n.* *(people)* A **person** is a man, woman, or child, a human being.

pet *n.* A **pet** is an animal that lives with people.

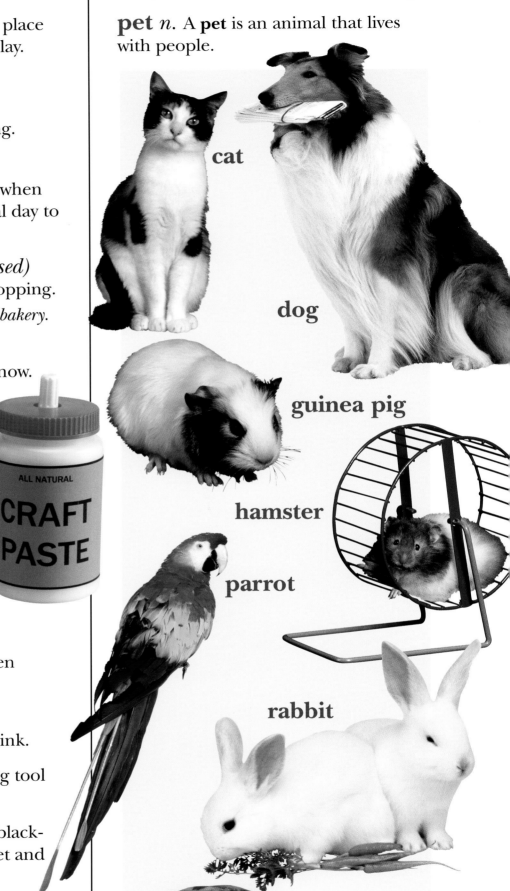

cat

dog

guinea pig

hamster

parrot

rabbit

turtle

A B C D E F G H I J K L M

petal *n.* A **petal** is the brightly colored leaf of a flower.

photograph *n.* A **photograph** is a picture taken by a camera.

picnic *n.* A **picnic** is a meal eaten outside.

picture *n.* A **picture** is a drawing, a painting, or a photograph.

pie *n.* **Pie** is a food covered in a crust and baked.

piece *n.* A **piece** is a part of something. *May I have a **piece** of pie?*

pile *n.* A **pile** is a lot of things that are put on top of each other. *My dirty clothes were thrown into a big **pile**.*

pill *n.* A **pill** is a little, round piece of solid medicine that is swallowed.

pillow *n.* A **pillow** is a soft cushion.

pin *n.* A **pin** is a small piece of metal that holds things together.

pirate *n.* **Pirates** are sailors who rob other ships at sea.

pizza *n.* A **pizza** is a food with a thin bread bottom that is covered with cheese and tomatoes and baked in the oven.

place¹ *n.* A **place** is somewhere where something can be found. *Our dog buries his bones in a **place** near the fence.*

place² *v.* **Place** also means put. ***Place** the napkins on the table, please.*

plain *adj.* **Plain** means simple. *I'm going to wear a **plain** red shirt.*

plan *v.* *(planned)* To **plan** is to think of how to do something. *Mom and I will **plan** Dad's birthday party.*

planet *n.* A **planet** is a large round body in space that travels around the Sun. *Mercury, Venus, Mars, and Jupiter are four of the nine **planets** in our solar system.*

plant¹ *n.* A **plant** is a living thing that grows out of the ground.

plant² *v.* **Plant** also means to put seeds in the ground so they will grow. *Every year my mom **plants** tomatoes in her garden.*

plastic *n.* **Plastic** is a strong, lightweight material that can be made into any shape. *Many toys are made of **plastic**.*

plate *n.* A **plate** is a flat dish for food.

play *v.* To **play** is to do something for fun.

please *adv.* **Please** is a polite word to use when you ask for something. *Dan, will you **please** pass the butter?*

N O P Q R S T U V W X Y Z

plus *prep.* **Plus** means and.
*Two **plus** two equals four.*

pocket *n.*
A **pocket** is sewn into your clothes and used for holding things.
*I keep my money in the **pocket** of my pants.*

poem *n.* A **poem** is a kind of writing that uses words in special ways.

point¹ *n.* A **point** is the sharp end of something.

point² *v.* **Point** also means to show where something is with your finger.
*Would you **point** to where the library is, please?*

police *n.* **Police** are people whose job is to make sure everyone obeys the law.

polite *adv.* You are **polite** when you are thinking about what other people would like you to do.
*It was only **polite** to thank Mary's mom for having the party.*

pond *n*
A **pond** is like a small lake.

pool *n.*
A **pool** is an area full of water.

poor *adj.* **Poor** means having very little money.

possible *adj.* **Possible** means something that can happen.

pot *n.* A **pot** is a deep round container we usually use for cooking.
*My mom made a big **pot** of delicious soup.*

pour *v.* **Pour** means to tip something so that the liquid inside falls out.

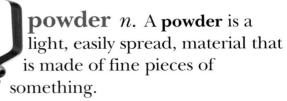

powder *n.* A **powder** is a light, easily spread, material that is made of fine pieces of something.
*We made everything look white by covering it up with chalk **powder**.*

power *n.*
Power means having strength.

practice *v.*
Practice means to do something over and over so you can learn to do it well.
*Evan **practices** piano after school.*

prepare *v.* Prepare means to get ready for something.
*We worked all morning to **prepare** for the picnic.*

present *n.*
A **present** is a gift.

pretend *v.* **Pretend** means to make-believe.
*Let's **pretend** we are flying in a spaceship.*

pretty *adj.* **Pretty** means nice to look at.

price *n.* **Price** is how much something costs.

prince *n.* A **prince** is the son of a king or queen.

princess *n. (princesses)* A **princess** is the daughter of a king and queen.

prize *n.* A **prize** is a gift given to the winner of a contest.

problem *n.* A **problem** is a question that we need to think about before we answer.
*Andy has a hard math **problem** to figure out.*

project *n.* A **project** is something you plan carefully and then do.

Mary's science project had taken three months to finish.

promise *v.* **Promise** means to keep your word.

I promise I will be home on time.

proud *adj.* **Proud** means feeling good about yourself.

I am proud that I won the race.

puddle *n.* A **puddle** is a little pool of water on the ground that forms after it rains.

pull *v.* **Pull** means to move something by bringing it towards you.

This door opens if you pull on the handle.

pumpkin *n.* A **pumpkin** is a round, orange fruit with very hard skin that grows on a vine.

Seeds from a pumpkin are delicious when they are toasted.

puppet *n.* A **puppet** is a doll that you can move with your hands or with strings.

push *v.* To **push** is to move something by pressing it away from you.

Uncle Dan pushed Tom in the stroller.

put *v.* **Put** means to set something down.

Please put your pencil on your desk.

puzzle *n.* A **puzzle** is a toy or game that gives you a problem that has to be solved.

Qq Rr

quarter *n.* A **quarter** is one of four equal parts of something.

Twenty-five cents is a quarter of a dollar.

queen *n.* A **queen** is a woman who rules a country or who is married to a king.

question *n.* A **question** is what you ask when you want to know something.

I raised my hand to ask a question about the lesson.

quick *adj.* **Quick** means fast.

quiet *adj.* **Quiet** means without noise.

race *n.* A **race** is a contest to see who is the fastest.

radio *n.* A **radio** is a machine that receives signals from the air and turns them into sounds like voices and music.

railroad *n.* A **railroad** is a track for trains made from bars of metal and wood.

rain *n.* **Rain** is drops of water that fall from the clouds.

rainbow *n.* A **rainbow** is a band of colors in the sky made by sunlight shining through raindrops.

reach *v.* **Reach** means to stretch out to touch or hold something.

I can't reach the shelf because it's too high.

reach *v.* **Reach** also means to get to where you are going.

Liz reached home in time for lunch.

read *v. (reads, reading, read)* To **read** means to be able to understand letters, words, and sentences.

ready *adj.* **Ready** means prepared or able to start.

Are you ready for bed?

real *adj.* **Real** means something that is not pretend.

Dragons are make-believe, but tigers are real.

reason *n.* A **reason** is an explanation for something.

The reason the ground is wet is because it rained last night.

refrigerator *n.* A **refrigerator** is a machine to keep food cold.

remember *v.* **Remember** means to think about something from the past.

I remember our trip to the circus last summer.

remind *v.* **Remind** means to tell someone to remember to do something.

Mom often reminds me not to bite my fingernails.

remove *v.* **Remove** means to take something away.

People come to remove our trash every Thursday.

repair *v.* **Repair** means to fix something that is broken.

Our washing machine wasn't working so Dad called someone to repair it.

reptile *n.* A **reptile** is a cold-blooded animal with scaly skin.

Lizards and turtles are reptiles.

alligator

chameleon

crocodile

iguanas

snake

turtle

rescue *v.* **Rescue** means to save someone from danger.
Lifeguards rescue people from drowning.

rest *v.* **Rest** means to stop working or moving when you are tired, to regain your strength.
After I clean up my room it will be time to rest.

restaurant *n.* A **restaurant** is a place where people go out to eat.

return *v.* To **return** is to go back to where you started out.

reward *n.* A **reward** is a prize for doing something especially good.
I received a reward for finding the puppy.

rhyme *n.* A **rhyme** is when words end in the same sound.
Rock and lock rhyme.

rice *n.* **Rice** is a cereal that people use for food.

rich *adj.*
Rich means having lots of money.

ride *v. (reads, riding, rode)* To **ride** means to sit on or in something that is moving.
My dog likes to ride in the wagon.

right¹ *adj.*
Right means correct.

right² *n.*
Right is also the opposite of left.

ring¹ *n.* A **ring** is a piece of jewelry worn around a finger.

ring² *v. (rings, ringing, rang, rung)* **Ring** also means to sound like a bell.
The school bell rings every morning.

river *n.* A **river** is a large body of moving water that flows from a high place to a lower place.
The land alongside a river is called a bank.

road *n.* A **road** is a street.

rock *n.* **Rock** is the hard material that the earth is made of.
Very large rocks are called boulders.

rocket *n.*
A **rocket** is a spaceship.

roll *v.* To **roll** something is to move it by turning it over and over.
Andy rolled the marble to Marcus.

roof *n.*
A **roof** is the outside top of a building.

room *n.* A **room** is an inside part of a building.

root *n.* A **root** is the part of a plant that grows under the ground.
Plants get water and food through their roots.

rough *adj.*
Rough means bumpy.

round *adj.* **Round** means in the shape of a circle.

row *n.*
A **row** is a group of things or people in a straight line.

rule¹ *n.* **Rules** tell people what behavior is allowed or not allowed.

rule² *v. (ruled, ruling)* To **rule** also means to lead a country or group of people.

run *v. (run, running, ran)* **Run** means to use your legs to move fast.

Ss

sad *adj.* **Sad** means unhappy.

safe *adj.* **Safe** means not in danger.
I feel safe at home.

sail/sailor *v., n.* To **sail** is to travel on a boat that is blown by the wind.
We are going to sail across the lake.

A **sailor** is someone who works on a ship or boat.

salad *n.* A **salad** is a mixture of raw fruits or vegetables.

salt *n.* **Salt** is a mineral used to flavor food.

same *adj.* **Same** means alike.
Mark and I have the same notebook.

sand *n.* **Sand** is tiny pieces of rock that have been ground down by the ocean.
The beach is covered in sand.

sandwich *n.* *(sandwiches)*
A **sandwich** is two pieces of bread with some kind of filling in the middle.

save¹ *v.* **Save** means to keep something for later.
I save my money in a piggy bank.

save² *v.* **Save** also means to rescue someone from danger.

say *v. (says, saying, said)* **Say** means to talk out loud.
What did he say about me?

scale *n.* A **scale** is a tool for weighing things.

scare *v.*
Scare means to frighten.

school *n.* A **school** is a place where students go to learn.

science *n.* **Science** is the study of the natural world.
In science class, we are learning how plants grow.

scissors *n.*
Scissors are a tool for cutting.

score *n.* The **score** is the number of points made by a team or player in a game.

scratch¹ *n. (scratches)*
A **scratch** is a cut.
I got a scratch on my arm from a sharp nail.

scratch² *v.* **Scratch** also means to make a mark with something sharp.
I used a nail to scratch a pattern on the wood.

scream *v.* To **scream** is to make a loud sound with your voice.

A B C D E F G H I J K L M

sea *n.* **Sea** is a large area of salt water, smaller than an ocean.

search *v.* To **search** is to look hard for something.

*Some scientists **search** for dinosaur bones.*

season *n.* A **season** is one of the four parts of the year.

*The **seasons** are called spring, summer, fall, and winter.*

second¹ *adj.* **Second** means the one after the first.

second² *n.* A **second** is also a tiny measure of time. Sixty seconds make one minute.

secret *n.* A **secret** is something that only a few people know.

*I told my best friend a **secret**.*

see *v. (sees, seeing, saw)* To **see** is to use your eyes to look at something.

*Can you **see** what the sign on the road says?*

seed *n.* A **seed** is the part of the plant that grows into a new plant.

sell *v. (sells, selling, sold)* **Sell** means to give something for money.

*Mikey **sells** lemonade for 25¢.*

send *v. (sends, sending, sent)* To **send** is to make someone or something go somewhere else.

*Don't forget to **send** Tom a birthday card.*

sew *v.* **Sew** means to join two things with a needle and thread.

*Will you **sew** the button on my shirt?*

shadow *n.* A **shadow** is the shade something makes when it blocks out the light.

*I can see my **shadow** on the sidewalk when it is sunny outside.*

shake *v. (shakes, shaking, shook)* **Shake** means to move something back and forth or up and down very fast.

***Shake** the bottle of juice before you open it.*

shape *n.* **Shape** is the outline of a form.

*I could tell it was a football by the **shape** of the package.*

share *v.* When you **share**, you let others have some of what is yours.

*I **share** my toys with my friends.*

shark *n.* A **shark** is a large fish with rows of very sharp teeth.

sharp *adj.* **Sharp** means having a pointed end or an edge that can cut things.

*Be careful, that knife is **sharp**.*

shell *n.* A **shell** is a hard covering that protects what is inside.

*Part of a turtle's body is a hard **shell**.*

shine *v. (shining, shined or shone)* **Shine** means to give off light.

*The Sun **shines** more brightly than any other light.*

ship *n.* A **ship** is a large boat.

shop¹ *n. (shops, shopping, shopped)* A **shop** is a place where things are sold or repaired.

shop² *v.* **Shop** means to buy things that you want or need.

*Mom and Dad **shop** for food every Saturday.*

N O P Q R **S** T U V W X Y Z

short *adj.*
Short means not tall or long.
*Cleo is wearing a **short** skirt.*

shout *v.* **Shout** means to talk in a very loud voice.
*David **shouts** when he is angry.*

show *v.* **Show** means to let others see something you have.
*Will you **show** the class the things you found on the beach yesterday?*

shower *v.* To **shower** is to wash while standing under running water.
*I **shower** before and after I go in a swimming pool.*

shut *v.*
Shut means to close something.
*Please **shut** the door.*

sick *adj.* **Sick** means not healthy.

side¹ *n.* A **side** is either the right or left of something.
*I write notes on the left **side** of my paper.*

side² *n.* **Side** also means the front or back of something that is flat.
*Use both **sides** of the paper to write your answers.*

sign *n.* A **sign** is a notice in words or pictures that gives information.

silver *n.* **Silver** is a valuable, shiny metal.

sing *v. (sings, singing, sang)*
To **sing** is to use your voice to make music.
*She **sang** into the microphone.*

sink¹ *v. (sinks, sinking, sank)* To **sink** means to disappear under water.
*If you throw a rock in the water, it will **sink** to the bottom.*

sink² *n.* A **sink** is something we use for washing up.
*I washed the dishes in the kitchen **sink**.*

sister *n.* A **sister** is a woman or girl who has the same parents as you.

sit *v. (sits, sitting, sat)* To **sit** means to rest on your bottom.
*George is **sitting** in the chair.*

size *n.* **Size** is how large or small something is.

skateboard *n.* A **skateboard** is a narrow board with little wheels on the bottom that you stand on to ride.

skeleton *n.* A **skeleton** is all the bones joined together inside the body.

skin *n.* **Skin** is the outside covering of a body.
*People have thin **skin**, but a rhinoceros has thick **skin**.*

sky *n. (skies)* The **sky** is the air above the earth.

sled *n.* A **sled** is something to sit on to ride over snow.

sleep *v. (sleep, sleeping, slept)*
Sleep means to close your eyes and rest your body and mind.

slice¹ *v.* **Slice** means to cut off a thin piece of something.
***Slice** the cake so everyone gets a piece.*

slice² *n.*
A **slice** is also a piece of something.
*May I have another **slice** of pie?*

slide *v. (slides, sliding, slid)*
Slide means to move easily over a slippery surface.
*When you ski, you **slide** on the snow.*

A B C D E F G H I J K L M

slip *v. (slips, slipping, slipped)*
Slip means to accidentally slide and then fall.

*Scott **slipped** on the ice and fell.*

slow *adj.* **Slow** means taking a long time to do something.

small *adj.* **Small** means little.

smart *adj.* **Smart** means able to learn things quickly.

*Chimps are very **smart** animals.*

smell *v.* **Smell** means to use your nose to find out about something.

*Can you **smell** what is cooking in the oven?*

smile *v.* To **smile** is to make a happy face by turning up the corners of your mouth.

smooth *adj.*
Smooth means not bumpy.

sneeze *n.* A **sneeze** is a sudden movement of air blown from your nose and mouth.

snow *n.* **Snow** is frozen water that falls from clouds.

soap *n.* **Soap** is something to wash and clean with.

soft *adj.* **Soft** means easy to press into.

*My pillow is very **soft**.*

solid *adj.* **Solid** means strong and hard.

*The walls of this building are **solid**.*

some *adj.* **Some** means an amount that is not exact.

*There are **some** hot dogs left, but I don't know how many.*

something *pron.*
Something means a thing that has not been named or described.

***Something** smells delicious.*

sometimes *adv.* **Sometimes** means once in a while.

***Sometimes** I like to be all by myself.*

somewhere *adv.* **Somewhere** means a place that is not known.

*I put my book **somewhere** and now I can't find it.*

song *n.* A **song** is music with words.

*They sang my favorite **song**.*

sorry *adj.*
Sorry means to feel bad about something.

*I am very **sorry** that I broke your crayon.*

sound *n.* A **sound** is something that you hear.

soup *n.* **Soup** is a hot or cold liquid food.

south *n.*
South is a direction. If you face where the sun comes up, **south** is on your right. It is the opposite of north.

space *n.*
Space means an empty place.

*There is **space** in this box for more books.*

Outer **space** is above the air in the sky. The other planets are in outer space.

speak *v. (speaks, speaking, spoke)*
Speak means to talk.

*Peter is **speaking** on his phone.*

special *adj.* **Special** means better in some way.

*This pen is **special** because it has three colors of ink.*

speed *n.* **Speed** is how fast something is moving.

spell *v.* **Spell** means to say the letters of a word in the correct order.

*You do not **spell** the word through the way it sounds.*

spend *v.* (spends, spending, spent) **Spend** means to use something up.

*How will you **spend** your money?*

spill *v.* To **spill** is when a liquid comes out of its container by accident.

*If you fill a glass too full, it may **spill**.*

spin *v.* (spins, spinning, spun) **Spin** means to turn around in circles very fast.

*Have you ever seen an ice skater **spin** on the ice?*

spoon *n.* A **spoon** is a tool used for eating or stirring.

sport *n.* A **sport** is a game that people play for fun.

*Baseball is a team **sport**.*

spot¹ *n.* A **spot** is a round mark.

*I can't wear this shirt because it has a **spot** on it.*

spot² *n.* A **spot** is also another word for a place.

*This is a nice **spot** to have a picnic.*

stair *n.* A **stair** is one of a set of steps used for going up or down.

stand *v.* (stands, standing, stood) When you **stand**, you are on your feet and not sitting.

*Clara is **standing**.*

star *n.* A **star** is a sun far away that we see in the night sky.

start *v.* **Start** means begin.

step¹ *n.* A **step** is the flat part of stairs or a ladder.

step² *v.* (steps, stepping, stepped) **Step** also means to lift your foot and put it down in another place.

*Please don't **step** on the cat!*

stick¹ *n.* A **stick** is a long, thin piece of wood.

stick² *v.* (sticks, sticking, stuck) **Stick** means to attach with glue or tape.

*Use tape to **stick** your picture to the wall.*

stir *v.* (stirs, stirring, stirred) **Stir** means to mix with a spoon.

*The chef **stirred** the cream.*

stone *n.* A **stone** is a piece of rock.

stop *v.* (stops, stopped, stopping) **Stop** means to not do something anymore.

*My watch **stopped** working at two o'clock.*

store *n.* A **store** is a place where you can buy things.

storm *n.* A **storm** is bad weather.

*There was thunder during the **storm**.*

story *n.* (stories) A **story** is telling about something that happened.

*A **story** can be real, or it can be made up.*

stove *n.* A **stove** is a machine used to heat and cook food.

straight *adj.* **Straight** means not having any bends or curves.

*It is hard to draw a **straight** line without a ruler.*

straw *n.*
Straw is the stems of dried plants.

street *n.* A **stree**t is a road.

string *n.* A **string** is a thin, strong thread for tying things up.

stripe *n.* A **stripe** is a straight band of color.

strong¹ *adj.* **Strong** means powerful.
*Michael is very **strong** and can lift heavy things.*

strong² *adj.* **Strong** also means hard and not easy to break.

subtract *v.*
Subtract means to take away.

sugar *n.* **Sugar** is a sweet flavoring for food and drinks.

suitcase *n.* A **suitcase** is a bag with a handle used for carrying clothes when traveling.

Sun *n.* The **Sun** is the closest star to Earth and is visible during the day.

surprise *n.* A **surprise** is something you did not know would happen.
*Getting a new puppy was a big **surprise**.*

sweep *v. (sweeps, sweeping, swept)* **Sweep** means to use a broom to clean the floor.
*I need to **sweep** the leaves off the porch.*

sweet *adj.*
Sweet means tasting like sugar.

swim *v. (swims, swimming, swam)* **Swim** means to use your arms and legs to move through water.
*I like to **swim** in the ocean.*

swing *v. (swings, swinging, swung)* **Swing** means to move back and forth through the air.
*We like to **swing** on the jungle gym.*

sword *n.* A **sword** is a very long, sharp knife with a handle at one end.
*A long time ago, **swords** were used as weapons.*

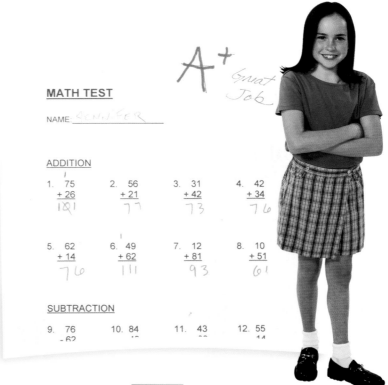

Tt

table *n.* A **table** is a piece of furniture with a flat top and legs.

tail *n.* A **tail** is the part of an animal that grows at the back of its body.
*A cat has a long **tail**.*

take *v. (takes, taking, took)* **Take** means to pick something up with your hand.
***Take** one piece of paper and pass the rest to the next person.*

talk *v.* **Talk** means to speak.

tall *adj.* **Tall** means high above the ground.
*Henry's dad is **tall**.*

taste *v.* **Taste** means to use your tongue to tell what something is like.

*Do you like to **taste** foods you have never tried before?*

tea *n.* **Tea** is a drink made by pouring boiling water on the dried leaves of a special plant.

teach *v.* *(teach, teaching, taught)* **Teach** means to help someone learn.

*Can you **teach** me to play the piano?*

teacher *n.*
A **teacher** is someone who teaches.

team *n.* A **team** is a group of people who work or play together.

tear¹ *v.* *(tears, tearing, tore)* **Tear** means to rip.

*If I **tear** my clothes, Mom will fix them for me.*

tear² *n.* A **tear** is a drop of salt water that falls from your eyes when you cry.

telephone *n.* A **telephone** is an instrument used for calling or speaking to someone in a different place.

television *n.* **Television** is a machine that turns signals from the air into pictures and sounds.

tell *v.* *(tells, telling, told)* **Tell** means to speak about something.

***Tell** me what you learned in school today.*

test *n.* A **test** is a way of finding out what someone knows.

thank *v.* **Thank** means to tell someone that they did a nice thing.

*Mom reminded me to **thank** my cousin for the present he gave me.*

thermometer *n.*
A **thermometer** is a tool for measuring heat or cold.

thick *adj.* **Thick** means wide.
*The walls of the fort are **thick**.*

thin *adj.* **Thin** is something with very little space between its sides.

thing *n.* **Things** are objects.

think *v.* *(thinks, thinking, thought)* **Think** means to use your brain to figure something out.

*Do you **think** you can put the puzzle together?*

thirsty *adj.* *(thirstier, thirstiest)* **Thirsty** means needing to drink something.

thread *n.* **Thread** is a very thin string used to sew things together.

through¹ *prep.* **Through** means going from one side of something to the other.

*Have you ever gone **through** a tunnel?*

through² *adj.*
Through also means finished.

*Are you **through** drawing your picture?*

throw *v.* *(throws, throwing, threw)* **Throw** means to use your arm to make something move through the air.

*The pitcher **throws** the ball to the catcher.*

thumb *n.* The **thumb** is the wide, powerful finger that closes against the other four fingers.

*Tanisha held the daisy between her **thumb** and middle finger.*

thunder *n.*
Thunder is a loud sound in the sky that you hear during a storm.

A B C D E F G H I J K L M

tie¹ *v. (tie, tying, tied)* **Tie** means to hold things together by making a knot in rope or string.

*I learned how to **tie** my shoes last year.*

tie² *n.* A **tie** is a long piece of cloth that hangs down the front of a shirt and is worn around the neck.

time *n.* **Time** is a measure of how long it takes to do something or for something to happen.

*It takes a long **time** to walk to school.*

tire *n.* A **tire** is a rubber wheel.

tired *adj.* **Tired** means ready to rest or sleep.

toaster *n.* A **toaster** is a small machine to heat and brown slices of bread.

today *n.* **Today** means this day.

tomorrow *n.* **Tomorrow** means the day after today.

tonight *n.* **Tonight** means this evening.

tool *n.* A **tool** is something you use to make or fix things.

*A saw is a good **tool** for cutting wood.*

tooth *n. (teeth)* A **tooth** is the hard, white, bony part that grows in rows in the mouth and is used to bite or chew food.

toothbrush *n.* A **toothbrush** is a small brush with a long handle used to clean our teeth

top *n.* The **top** is the highest part of something

touch *v.* **Touch** means to use your hand or another body part to feel something.

towel *n.* A **towel** is a soft cloth used for drying.

toy *n.* A **toy** is something to be played with.

train *n.* A **train** is a group of railroad cars that run on a track.

treasure *n.* **Treasure** is something valuable.

tree *n.* A **tree** is a large plant with strong roots and a thick wooden trunk.

trick *n.* A **trick** is something you say or do that fools people.

tricycle *n.* A **tricycle** is a bike with two wheels in the back and one larger wheel in the front.

trip *n.* To take a **trip** is to travel somewhere.

trouble *n.* To be in **trouble** is to have done something that upset someone or that you may be punished for.

*I was in **trouble** for not coming right home after school.*

truck *n.* A **truck** is a vehicle with lots of room in the back for carrying things.

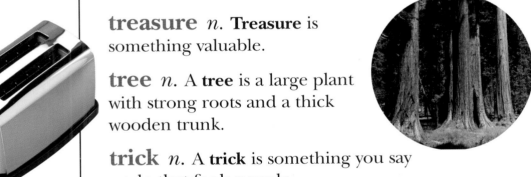
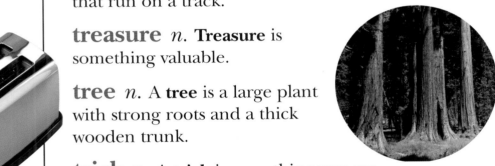
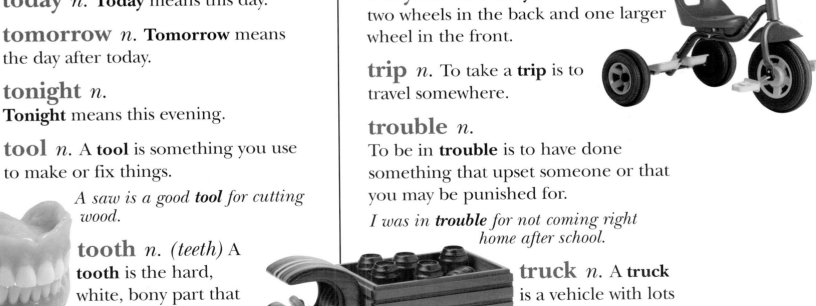

N O P Q R S **T** U V W X Y Z

true *adj.*
True means correct or real.

*It is **true** that Louis is seven years old.*

trunk¹ *n.*
A **trunk** is the center of a tree that grows from the ground.

trunk² *n.* A **trunk** is also an elephant's nose.

*An elephant uses its **trunk** to pick up things.*

truth *n.* The **truth** is something that is true.

try¹ *v. (tries, trying, tried)* **Try** means to see if you can do something.

*I am going to **try** to lift this weight.*

try² *v. (tries, trying, tried)* **Try** also means to see if you like something.

*Do you want to **try** this new cereal?*

tube *n.*
A **tube** is a long hollow container used for holding things.

*I squeezed the **tube** of toothpaste.*

SODIUM FLUORIDE AN

tulip *n.* A **tulip** is a long-stemmed flower that grows from a bulb and blooms in the spring.

***Tulips** come in many beautiful colors.*

tunnel *n.* A **tunnel** is an underground path.

turn *v.* **Turn** means to move in a different direction.

twice *adv.* **Twice** means two times.

twin *n.* A **twin** is one of two people or animals who are born at the same time.

Uu Vv Ww

ugly *adj.*
Ugly means not nice to look at.

*Some people think baboons are **ugly**, but I don't agree.*

umbrella *n.* An **umbrella** is a round cover made from cloth or plastic attached to a long handle, used to protect us from rain or sunlight. Umbrellas fold around their handles when we don't need them.

uncle *n.*
Your **uncle** is a brother of one of your parents, or your aunt's husband.

under *adv.*
Under means below something.

understand *v. (understands, understanding, understood)* To **understand** is to know about something.

up *adv.* **Up** means to go from a lower place to a higher place.

*The dancer went **up** on her toes.*

upset *v. (upset, upsetting)* **Upset** means unhappy, worried, mad, or sad.
*I was **upset** when I broke my watch.*

use *adj. (use, using, used)* **Use** means to have help from something to do a job.
*I **use** a vacuum to clean the rugs.*

valley *n.* A **valley** is the low land between mountains or hills.

valuable *adj.* **Valuable** means worth a lot.
*My mother's jewelry is very **valuable**.*

vegetable *n.* A **vegetable** is a plant grown for food.
*Carrots and broccoli are **vegetables**.*

asparagus

broccoli

carrots

cucumbers

corn

green beans

mushrooms

lettuce

onions

potatoes

visit *v.* **Visit** means to go to see someone or something for a while.
*I **visit** my grandmother for two weeks each summer.*

vitamin *n.* **Vitamins** are special things our bodies need to grow and stay healthy.
*We take our **vitamins** every morning with breakfast.*

wagon *n.* A **wagon** is a small, open cart with four wheels and a handle for pulling it.
*I pulled my **wagon** full of toys to my friend's house.*

wait *v.* **Wait** means to stay in one place for a reason.
*We had to **wait** an hour to get on the ride.*

waiter *n.* A **waiter** is the person who brings you the food in a restaurant.
*A female **waiter** is called a waitress.*

walk *v.* **Walk** means to move along on your feet.
*I **walk** to school every morning.*

wall *n.* A **wall** is one side of a building or room.

want *v.* To **want** means you would like to have or do something.
*I **want** to have spaghetti for dinner.*

warm *adj.* **Warm** means closer to hot than cold.
*My coat keeps me **warm**.*

wash *v.* **Wash** means to make something clean.
*Please **wash** your hands before dinner.*

waste *v.* **Waste** means to use or take more of something than you need.
*Use both sides of the paper so you don't **waste** it.*

N O P Q R S T U **V** W X Y Z

watch[1] *n. (watches)* A **watch** is a very small clock worn on the wrist.

watch[2] *v.* **Watch** means to look at something carefully.

water *n.* **Water** is a clear liquid that comes from rain or melting snow. It has no taste or smell.

wave[1] *v.* To **wave** means to move your arm and hand from side to side.

*My baby sister can **wave** and say "bye-bye."*

wave[2] *n.* A **wave** is a part of the ocean that rolls towards the beach.

weak *adj.* **Weak** means not strong.

*My legs felt **weak** after climbing so many stairs.*

wear *v. (wears, wearing, wore)* To **wear** something means to put it on your body.

*Lisa is **wearing** a purple shirt and white pants.*

weather *n.* **Weather** is what it is like outside.

*This week the **weather** has been cold and cloudy.*

week *n.* A **week** is made up of seven days.

weigh *v.* **Weigh** means to use a scale to find out how heavy something is.

*Please **weigh** these apples for me.*

west *n.* **West** is the direction where the Sun goes down. It is the opposite of east.

wet *adj. (wet, wetter, wettest)* **Wet** means soaked with water.

*The rain made my hair **wet**.*

whale *n.* A **whale** is a huge mammal that lives in the ocean.

what *pron.* **What** is a word used to ask which thing or which one.

***What** are we having for lunch?*

wheat *n.* **Wheat** is a tall grass used to make flour for bread, cereals, and pasta.

*Dad has a bowl of **wheat** flakes for breakfast everyday.*

wheel *n.* A **wheel** is something that turns around and around to make things move.

*My bicycle has two **wheels**.*

wheelchair *n.* A **wheelchair** is a special chair with wheels that you use if you are not able to walk.

whisper *v.* **Whisper** means to speak very softly.

*If you need to talk in a library, you should **whisper**.*

whistle[1] *n.* A **whistle** is a small instrument that makes a loud sound when blown.

whistle[2] *v.* To **whistle** means to make a high sound by blowing air through your lips or teeth.

whole *adj.* **Whole** means not missing any of its parts.

*Billy told the **whole** story.*

wide *adj.* **Wide** means a big distance from one side to the other.

*This highway is **wide** enough for eight lanes of cars.*

wife *n. (wives)* A **wife** is a married woman.

*Sally is Frank's **wife**.*

wild *adj*. **Wild** means growing or living in nature without help from people.

*Lions and tigers are **wild** animals.*

wild animals

chimpanzee

deer

elephant

kangaroo

leopard

lion

racoon

skunk

win *v. (wins, winning, won)* **Win** means to be the best at a game or a contest.

*Rosie hopes to **win** the spelling bee his year.*

wind *n*. **Wind** is moving air.

window *n*. A **window** is an opening in a wall of a building that lets in light and air.

*Most **windows** are made of glass.*

wing *n*. A **wing** is the part of a bird's body used for flying. Airplanes also have wings.

wish *v*. **Wish** means to want something very much.

*I **wish** I could be an astronaut.*

woman *n. (women)* A **woman** is a grown-up female person.

wood *n*. **Wood** is what trees are made of.

wool *n*. **Wool** is yarn that is made from the hair of goats and sheep.

*My blanket is made of **wool**.*

word *n*. A **word** is a group of letters or sounds that mean something in a language.

work¹ *v*. To **work** is to do a job.

work² *n*. **Work** is also the energy we use to get something done.

*It was a lot of **work** to paint the porch.*

world *n*. The **world** is our planet Earth and everyone and everything on it.

worm *n*. A **worm** is a small animal with a soft body that lives in the ground.

worry *v. (worries, worrying, worried)* **Worry** means to be afraid that something bad might happen.

*Andy always **worries** before he takes a test.*

worst *adj.*
Worst is the opposite of best.
*That was the **worst** movie I ever saw!*

wrap *v.* *(wraps, wrapping, wrapped)* **Wrap** means to cover something completely.
*Use the blue paper to **wrap** Bill's birthday present.*

write *v.* *(writes, writing, wrote)* **Write** means to put letters or numbers on paper so they can be read.
*Did you **write** your book report yet?*

wrong *adj.* **Wrong** means not correct or true.

Xx Yy Zz

x-ray *n.* An **x-ray** is a picture taken by a special machine that shows the inside of the body.
*The doctor knew my bone was broken after he saw the **x-ray** of my chest.*

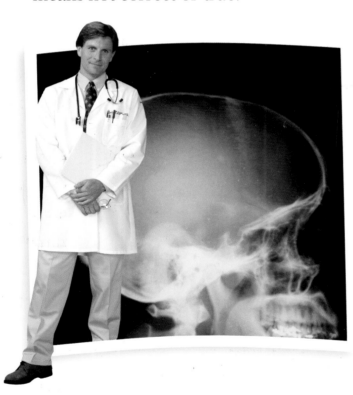

yawn *v.* **Yawn** means to open your mouth wide and take in a deep breath.
*I **yawn** when I am sleepy.*

year *n.* A **year** is 365 days.
*Another way to measure a **year** is to say that it has 12 months or 52 weeks.*

yell *v.* **Yell** means shout.
*It was so noisy that we had to **yell** to be heard.*

yes *adv.*
Yes is what we say when we agree.

yesterday *n.* **Yesterday** means the day before today.

yogurt *n.* **Yogurt** is a soft, thick food made from milk that is often flavored with fruit.

yolk *n.* A **yolk** is the yellow part of an egg.

young *adj.* **Young** means not old.
*My dog isn't a puppy anymore, but he is still very **young**.*

zebra *n.* A **zebra** is a wild animal that looks like a black and white striped horse.

zero *n.* **Zero** is the word for the number 0.
*One plus **zero** equals one.*

zipper *n.* A **zipper** is two strips of metal or plastic teeth that lock together when closed and come apart when open.
*It was getting cold, so I closed the **zipper** on my jacket.*

zoo *n.* A **zoo** is a place where animals are kept so people can learn about them.